the COMPLETE
DIY COOKBOOK
for YOUNG CHEFS

make the mix so that you can have waffles anytime!

add your favorite topping!

AMERICA'S
TEST KITCHEN

OTHER COOKBOOKS BY AMERICA'S TEST KITCHEN KIDS

The Complete Cookbook for Young Chefs
#1 *New York Times* best seller, 2019 IACP Cookbook Award Winner for Children, Youth & Family

The Complete Baby and Toddler Cookbook
2020 IACP Cookbook Award Nominee for Children, Youth & Family

The Complete Baking Book for Young Chefs
New York Times best seller, 2020 IACP Cookbook Award Nominee for Children, Youth & Family

My First Cookbook

PRAISE FOR AMERICA'S TEST KITCHEN KIDS

"The inviting, encouraging tone, which never talks down to the audience; emphasis on introducing and reinforcing basic skills; and approachable, simplified recipes make this a notable standout among cookbooks for kids." —*Booklist*, starred review, on *The Complete Cookbook for Young Chefs*

"a must-have book . . . a great holiday buy, too." —*School Library Journal*, on *The Complete Cookbook for Young Chefs*

"Inspiring not just a confidence in executing delicious recipes but encouraging them to build foundational kitchen skills." —The Takeout, on *The Complete Cookbook for Young Chefs*

"What a great way to encourage a child to find fun in the kitchen!" —Tribune Content Agency, on *The Complete Cookbook for Young Chefs*

"The perfect gift . . . Any kid who spends enough time with this book will learn enough to at least make their own school lunches—if not the occasional family meal." —Epicurious, on *The Complete Cookbook for Young Chefs*

"For kids who are interested in cooking . . . [*The Complete Cookbook for Young Chefs*] introduces kids to all the basics . . . and of course there's a whole lot of easy and very tasty recipes to try." —NPR's *Morning Edition*, on *The Complete Cookbook for Young Chefs*

Library of Congress Cataloging-in-Publication Data

Names: America's Test Kitchen (Firm), author.
Title: The complete diy cookbook for young chefs / America's Test Kitchen Kids.
Description: Boston, MA : America's Test Kitchen, [2020] | Includes index. | Audience: Ages 8-12. | Audience: Grades 4-6.
Identifiers: LCCN 2020019196 (print) | LCCN 2020019197 (ebook) | ISBN 9781948703246 (hardcover) | ISBN 9781948703253 (ebook)
Subjects: LCSH: Cooks--Juvenile literature. | Cooking--Juvenile literature. | CYAC: Cookbooks. lcgft
Classification: LCC TX652.5 .A457 2020 (print) | LCC TX652.5 (ebook) | DDC 641.5092--dc23
LC record available at https://lccn.loc.gov/2020019196
LC ebook record available at https://lccn.loc.gov/2020019197

America's Test Kitchen

21 Drydock Avenue, Boston, MA 02210

Manufactured in the United States of America

Distributed by Penguin Random House Publisher Services

Tel: 800.733.3000

Front Cover Photograph:
Kevin White and Catrine Kelty

AMERICA'S TEST KITCHEN

Editor in Chief: Molly Birnbaum

Executive Food Editor: Suzannah McFerran

Senior Editors: Afton Cyrus, Sarah Wilson

Test Cooks: Andrea Wawrzyn, Amanda Luchtel

Deputy Editor, Education: Kristin Sargianis

Assistant Editor: Katy O'Hara

Photography Director: Julie Cote

Design Director: Lindsey Timko Chandler

Designer: Jen Kanavos Hoffman

Photographer: Kevin White

Food Styling: Ashley Moore, Elle Simone Scott, Kendra Smith

Photography Producer: Meredith Mulcahy

Photo Shoot Kitchen Team:

Test Kitchen Director: Erin McMurrer

Managers: Alli Berkey, Tim McQuinn

Lead Test Cook: Eric Haessler

Test Cooks: Hannah Fenton, Jacqueline Gochenouer, Gina McCreadie, Christa West

Senior Manager, Publishing Operations: Taylor Argenzio

Imaging Manager: Lauren Robbins

Production and Imaging Specialists: Dennis Noble, Tricia Neumyer, Amanda Yong

Copy Editors: Christine Campbell, April Poole, Rachel Schowalter

Chief Creative Officer: Jack Bishop

Executive Editorial Directors: Julia Collin Davison, Bridget Lancaster

contents

introduction

Food Tastes Better When You *Do It Yourself* (DIY) at Home!
Cooking is cool. Baking is awesome. But this book brings something even
better to the table: recipes to make your favorite store-bought items—from
ketchup to sprinkles to pancake mix—FROM SCRATCH! These recipes
are perfect for everything from a weekend project with your family to an
after-school snack to homemade gifts for the holidays.

This book, like our first two books for kids ages 8 to 13—*The Complete
Cookbook for Young Chefs* and *The Complete Baking Book for Young
Chefs*—is kid tested and kid approved. That means that there are thousands
of other kids just like you out there, making these recipes and sharing them
with their friends and family, loving the process and the results. When we
were making this book, we had more than 7,000 kids testing each and
every recipe, sending us feedback (and even coming into our office to
cook in the test kitchen!), and letting us know what worked well and what
could use improvement. You'll see a handful of these recipe testers in the
pages of this book. Thank you to everyone who helped make this book as
delicious as possible!

Cooking and baking, whether something new or something familiar, is a
science as well as an art. Don't be surprised if you have questions as you
begin to operate in the kitchen on your own (never hesitate to ask a grown-
up!) and if you make some mistakes (we've all been there many times).
Mistakes are an important part of the kitchen-learning process. But the most
important part as you begin cooking is to have fun! Use this book to be
creative, to try out new things, and to experiment. Be proud of everything
you accomplish.

READY, SET, DIY!

UNDERSTANDING THE SYMBOLS IN THIS BOOK

To help you find the right recipe for you, this book relies on a system of symbols to designate skill level as well as type of cooking required.

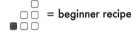 = beginner recipe

 = intermediate recipe

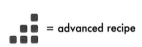 = advanced recipe

 = requires use of knife

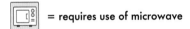 = requires use of microwave

 = requires use of stovetop

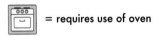 = requires use of oven

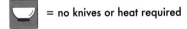 = no knives or heat required

HOW TO USE THE RECIPES IN THIS BOOK

Cooking from a recipe is actually a three-step process, and the recipes in this book are written to reflect that, with three distinct sections. The key to successful (and easy!) cooking is, in our humble opinion, all about organization. If you prepare all your ingredients (do the chopping or measuring or melting) and gather all your equipment before you start cooking, then you won't have to run around the kitchen looking for that last pan or hectically measure out that last cup of flour (or, worse, realize that you're out of flour!).

PREPARE INGREDIENTS

Start with the list of ingredients and prepare them as directed. Measure ingredients, melt butter, and chop as needed. Wash fruits and vegetables. You can use small prep bowls to keep ingredients organized.

GATHER COOKING EQUIPMENT

Once all your ingredients are ready, put all the tools you will need to follow the recipe instructions on the counter.

START COOKING!

It's finally time to start cooking. Any ingredients that need to be prepped at the last minute will have instructions within the recipe itself. Don't forget to have fun!

Cooking is not rocket science. Humans have been cooking since we learned to control fire more than one million years ago. What cooking does require is attention to detail. Here are four secrets to becoming a kitchen pro.

SECRET #1
READ CAREFULLY

If you're learning to cook, chances are you are starting with a recipe. It will take some time to understand the language used in recipes (see "Decoding Kitchenspeak," page 10).

Start with the key stats. How much food does the recipe make? How long will it take? When you're hungry for an after-school snack, choose a recipe that takes 15 to 30 minutes to prepare rather than an hour or two.

Make sure that you have the right ingredients and equipment. Don't start a ketchup recipe only to realize that there are no tomatoes in your kitchen. Likewise, don't prepare the ingredients for ice cream or ice pops before making sure that you have the right equipment.

Follow the recipe as written, at least the first time. You can always improvise once you understand how the recipe works. See the "Try It This Way" and "Use It This Way" sidebars for suggestions on how to customize recipes to suit your taste.

SECRET #2
STAY FOCUSED

Cooking requires the active participation of the cook.

Measure carefully (see page 13 for tips). Too much salt can ruin a recipe. Too little baking powder and your cake doesn't rise.

Recipes are written with both visual cues ("Cook until golden brown") and times ("Cook for 5 minutes"). Good cooks use all their senses—sight, hearing, touch, smell, and taste—in the kitchen.

Many recipes contain time ranges, such as "Cook until brown, 20 to 25 minutes." These ranges account for differences in various stovetops or ovens. Set your timer for the lower number. If the food isn't done when the timer goes off, you can always keep cooking and reset the timer. But once food is overcooked, there's no going back.

SECRET #3
PRACTICE SAFETY

Yes, knives and stoves can be dangerous. Always ask for help if you're in doubt.

Use the knife that's right for you. This will depend on the size of your hands and your skill level.

Hot stovetops and ovens can cause painful burns. Assume that anything on the stovetop (including the pan's handle and lid) is hot. Everything inside the oven is definitely hot. Always use oven mitts when using the oven.

Wash your hands before cooking.

Wash your hands after touching raw meat, chicken, fish, or eggs.

Never let foods you eat raw (such as berries) touch foods you will cook (such as eggs).

Don't ever leave something on the stove unattended. Always turn off the stove and oven when you're done.

SECRET #4
MISTAKES ARE OK

Making mistakes is a great way to learn. Don't sweat it.

Try to figure out what you would do differently next time. Maybe you should have set a timer so that you would remember to check the cookies in the oven. Maybe you should have measured more carefully.

If your food isn't perfect, don't worry. A misshapen cookie is still delicious. If you enjoy your "mistakes," everyone else will enjoy them, too. Remember: You cooked! That's so cool.

DECODING KITCHENSPEAK

Reading a recipe can sometimes feel like reading a foreign language. Here are some common words in many cookbooks and what they really mean.

THINGS YOU DO WITH A SHARP TOOL

PEEL   To remove the outer skin, rind, or layer from food, usually a piece of fruit or a vegetable. Often done with a vegetable peeler.

ZEST   To remove the flavorful colored outer peel from a lemon, lime, or orange (the colored skin is called the zest). Does not include the bitter white layer (called the pith) under the zest.

CHOP   To cut food with a knife into small pieces. Chopped fine = ⅛- to ¼-inch pieces. Chopped = ¼- to ½-inch pieces. Chopped coarse = ½- to ¾-inch pieces. Use a ruler to understand the different sizes.

MINCE   To cut food with a knife into ⅛-inch pieces or smaller.

SLICE   To cut food with a knife into pieces with two flat sides, with the thickness dependent on the recipe instructions. For example, slicing a celery stalk.

GRATE   To cut food (often cheese) into very small, uniform pieces using a rasp grater or the small holes on a box grater.

SHRED   To cut food (often cheese but also some vegetables and fruits) into small, uniform pieces using the large holes on a box grater or the shredding disk of a food processor.

THINGS YOU DO IN A BOWL

STIR   To combine ingredients in a bowl or cooking vessel, often with a rubber spatula or wooden spoon.

TOSS   To gently combine ingredients with tongs or two forks and/or spoons in order to distribute the ingredients evenly. You toss salad in a bowl (you don't stir it).

WHISK   To combine ingredients with a whisk until uniform or evenly incorporated. For example, you whisk whole eggs before scrambling them.

BEAT   To combine vigorously with a whisk, fork, or electric mixer, often with the goal of adding air to increase the volume of the ingredients (such as beating butter and sugar together to make cookie dough).

WHIP   To combine vigorously with a whisk or electric mixer, with the goal of adding air to increase the volume of the ingredients (such as whipping cream or egg whites).

SCRAPE   To push ingredients on the sides of a bowl, pan, blender jar, or food processor back to the center. A rubber spatula is the best tool for this job.

THINGS YOU DO WITH HEAT

MELT To heat solid food (think butter) on the stovetop or in the microwave until it becomes a liquid.

HEAT UNTIL SHIMMERING To heat oil in a pan until it begins to move slightly, which indicates the oil is hot enough for cooking. If the oil starts to smoke, it has been overheated, and you should start over with fresh oil.

SIMMER To heat liquid until small bubbles gently break the surface at a variable and infrequent rate, as when cooking a soup.

BOIL To heat liquid until large bubbles break the surface at a rapid and constant rate, as when cooking pasta.

TOAST To heat food (often nuts or bread) in a skillet, toaster, or oven until golden brown and fragrant.

WHAT'S UP WITH INGREDIENTS?

A well-stocked pantry means you are ready to cook.
Here are items to keep on hand, with notes on what to buy.

SALT There are many kinds of salt. Recipes in this book were tested with table salt (the kind with fine crystals that you can keep in a shaker). You can use larger, chunkier kosher salt or sea salt, but you will need a bit more of it.

PEPPER Whole peppercorns freshly ground in a pepper mill are much more flavorful than the ground pepper you buy in the supermarket.

OIL Use extra-virgin olive oil in recipes where the flavor of the oil is important, such as salad dressing. Flavorless vegetable oil is useful in many cooking and baking recipes. We also use coconut oil in some of our recipes.

BUTTER Use unsalted butter. Salted butter is great on toast but can make some foods too salty.

EGGS Most recipes call for large eggs. You can use different sizes in egg dishes (such as an omelet), but for all baking recipes in this book use large eggs.

MILK & DAIRY Milk, cream, half-and-half, yogurt, and sour cream are common ingredients. While low-fat milk and whole milk will work the same way in most recipes, don't use milk in a recipe that calls for cream. To help make our DIY mixes, we also often use milk, buttermilk, and even cheese that have been turned into a powder.

HERBS Fresh herbs add so much more flavor to dishes than dried ones. Dried oregano and thyme are OK, but don't bother with dried parsley, basil, or cilantro (they taste like sawdust).

SPICES Ground spices, such as cumin and chili powder, add flavor in a flash. Keep spices in the pantry for up to one year, and then buy fresh jars.

GARLIC & ONIONS
Many savory recipes call for garlic and/or onions. These flavorful ingredients require special prep (see page 17) and should be stored in the pantry, not the refrigerator.

BAKING POWDER & BAKING SODA These leaveners are essential in pancakes, muffins, cakes, cookies, and more. They are not interchangeable.

FLOUR Stock all-purpose flour in your pantry—it works well in a wide range of recipes, from cakes to cookies. In this book we also use whole-wheat flour (or, if you want, graham flour).

SUGAR Granulated white sugar is the most commonly used sweetener, although some recipes call for confectioners' (powdered) sugar or brown sugar (light or dark).

COCOA POWDER
There are a few different kinds of cocoa powder used to add deep chocolate flavor to cookies and cakes. Most often we use Dutch-processed. For special recipes (such as our Chocolate Sandwich Cookies) we use black cocoa powder.

HOW TO MEASURE AND WEIGH

For consistent cooking results, it's important to measure accurately. There are two ways to measure ingredients: by weight, using a scale, or by volume, using measuring cups and spoons. Using a scale to weigh your ingredients is the most accurate. But if you do not have a scale, that's OK! Below are tips on using a scale and how best to measure ingredients if you do not have a scale.

USING A SCALE

Turn on the scale and place the bowl on the scale. Then press the "tare" button to zero out the weight (that means that the weight of the bowl won't be included!).

Slowly add your ingredient to the bowl until you reach the desired weight. Here we are weighing 5 ounces of all-purpose flour (which is equal to 1 cup).

HOW TO MEASURE DRY AND LIQUID INGREDIENTS

Dry ingredients and liquid ingredients are measured differently. Note that small amounts of both dry and liquid ingredients are measured with small measuring spoons.

Dry ingredients should be measured in dry measuring cups—small metal or plastic cups with handles. Each set has cups of varying sizes. Dip the measuring cup into the ingredient and sweep away the excess with the back of a butter knife.

Liquid ingredients (milk, water, juice) should be measured in a liquid measuring cup (a larger, clear plastic or glass cup with lines on the side, a big handle, and a pour spout). Set the measuring cup level on the counter and bend down to read the bottom of the concave arc at the liquid's surface. This is known as the meniscus line.

KITCHEN MATH

You can get carried away learning all the math behind measuring. Memorize the following rules, and you will be all set.

3 TEASPOONS = 1 TABLESPOON

16 TABLESPOONS = 1 CUP

16 OUNCES = 1 POUND

13

ESSENTIAL PREP STEPS

HOW TO MELT BUTTER

Butter can be melted in a small saucepan on the stove (use medium-low heat), but we think the microwave is easier.

1. Cut butter into 1-tablespoon pieces. Place butter in microwave-safe bowl. Cover bowl with small plate.

2. Place in microwave. Heat butter at 50 percent power until melted, 30 to 60 seconds (longer if melting a lot of butter). Watch butter and stop microwave as soon as butter has melted. Use oven mitts to remove bowl from microwave.

HOW TO SOFTEN BUTTER

When taken straight from the refrigerator, butter is quite firm. For some baking recipes, you need to soften butter before trying to combine it with other ingredients. This is just a fancy term for letting the temperature of butter rise from 35 degrees (its refrigerator temperature) to 65 degrees (cool room temperature). This takes about 1 hour. But here are two ways to speed things up.

Counter Method: Cut butter into 1-inch pieces (to create more surface area). Place butter on plate and wait about 30 minutes. Once butter gives to light pressure (try to push your fingertip into butter), it's ready to use.

Microwave Method: Cut butter into 1-inch pieces and place on microwave-safe plate. Heat in microwave at 50 percent power for 10 seconds. Check butter with fingertip test. Heat for another 5 to 10 seconds if necessary.

HOW TO CRACK AND SEPARATE EGGS

Unless you are hard-cooking eggs, you need to start by cracking them open. In some recipes, you will need to separate the yolk (the yellow part) and the white (the clear part) and use them differently. Cold eggs are much easier to separate.

1. To crack: Gently hit side of egg against flat surface of counter or cutting board.

2. Pull shell apart into 2 pieces over bowl. Let yolk and white drop into bowl. Discard shell.

3. To separate yolk and white: Use your hand to very gently transfer yolk to second bowl.

HOW TO GRATE OR SHRED CHEESE

Cheese is often cut into very small pieces to flavor pizza, bread, rolls, and more. When grating or shredding, use a big piece of cheese so that your hand stays safely away from the sharp holes.

1. To grate: Hard cheeses such as Parmesan can be rubbed against a rasp grater or the small holes of a box grater to make a fluffy pile of cheese.

2. To shred: Semisoft cheeses such as cheddar or mozzarella can be rubbed against the large holes of a box grater to make long pieces of cheese.

HOW TO CHOP FRESH HERBS

Fresh herbs need to be washed and dried before they are chopped (or minced).

1. Use your fingers to remove leaves from stems; discard stems.

2. Gather leaves into small pile. Place 1 hand on handle of chef's knife and rest fingers of your other hand on top of blade. Use rocking motion, pivoting knife as you chop.

HOW TO ZEST AND JUICE CITRUS FRUIT

The flavorful colored skin from lemons, limes, and oranges (called the zest) is often removed and used in recipes. If you need zest, it's best to zest before juicing. After juicing, use a small spoon to remove any seeds from the bowl of juice.

1. To zest: Rub fruit against rasp grater to remove colored zest. Turn fruit as you go to avoid bitter white layer underneath zest.

2. To juice: Cut fruit in half through equator (not through ends).

3. Place 1 half of fruit in citrus juicer. Hold juicer over bowl and squeeze to extract juice.

HOW TO MINCE GARLIC

Garlic is sticky, so you may need to carefully wipe the pieces of garlic from the sides of the knife to get them back onto the cutting board, where you can cut them. You can also use a garlic press to both crush and mince garlic—so easy.

1. Crush clove with bottom of measuring cup to loosen papery skin. Use your fingers to remove and discard papery skin.

2. Place 1 hand on handle of chef's knife and rest fingers of your other hand on top of blade. Use rocking motion, pivoting knife as you chop garlic repeatedly to cut it into very small pieces.

HOW TO CHOP ONIONS OR SHALLOTS

Shallots are smaller, milder cousins to onions. If working with a small shallot, there's no need to cut it in half.

1. Halve onion through root end, then use your fingers to remove peel. Trim top of onion.

2. Place onion half flat side down. Starting 1 inch from root end, make several vertical cuts.

3. Rotate onion and slice across first cuts. As you slice, onion will fall apart into chopped pieces.

HOW TO GREASE A BAKING PAN OR MUFFIN TIN

In most recipes, pans need just a quick coat of vegetable oil spray and they are ready to go. Try this trick to keep mess to a minimum.

Hold baking pan or muffin tin over sink. Spray inside of pan, making sure to get even coverage on bottom and sides. Don't worry if some spray misses the mark. It will wash off the next time you wash dishes.

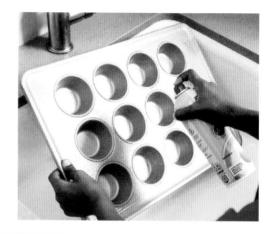

HOW TO TEST FOR DONENESS WITH A TOOTHPICK

Here's an easy way to test baked goods (muffins, cakes, brownies, and more) for doneness. See individual recipes—in some cases the toothpick should come out clean, while in other recipes a few crumbs are OK. If you see wet, sticky batter, keep on baking.

Insert toothpick into center of baked good, then remove it. Examine toothpick for crumbs and evaluate it against directions in recipe to determine if baked good is ready to come out of oven.

clean

crumbs attached

HOW TO FILL A PASTRY BAG

Pastry bags and tips are often used to pipe elaborate decorations on cakes. But they are also helpful for other things like our Sprinkles (see page 148).

1. Use scissors to cut 2½ inches off bottom corner of pastry bag.

2. Fold top of pastry bag out and halfway down.

3. Insert decorating tip all the way into bag so tip is peeking out of snipped bag corner.

4. Stand bag upright in drinking glass (with tip touching bottom of glass). Use rubber spatula to transfer icing to bag.

5. Twist top of bag nice and tight to push icing down toward tip. There should be no air between icing and top of bag.

TOOLS TO MAKE THE WORK EASIER

The right kitchen gear is essential. Here are the tools you will use over and over again. We've divided items into six categories: small appliances, knives, cookware and bakeware, kitchen basics, prep tools, and cooking and baking tools.

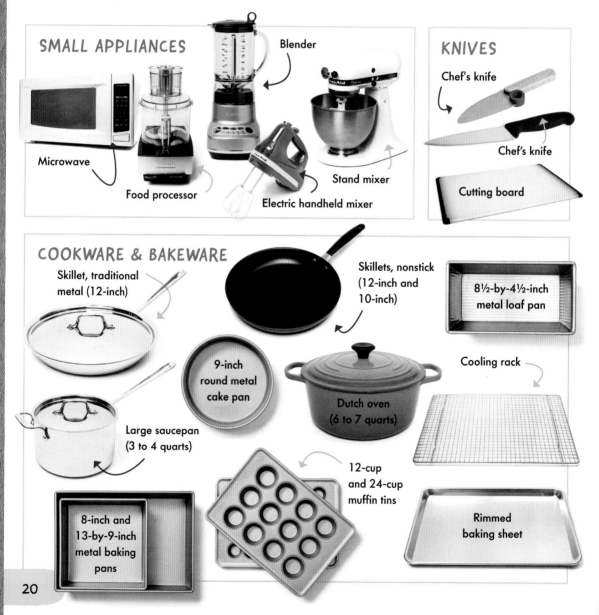

SMALL APPLIANCES

Blender

Microwave

Food processor

Electric handheld mixer

Stand mixer

KNIVES

Chef's knife

Chef's knife

Cutting board

COOKWARE & BAKEWARE

Skillet, traditional metal (12-inch)

Skillets, nonstick (12-inch and 10-inch)

8½-by-4½-inch metal loaf pan

9-inch round metal cake pan

Dutch oven (6 to 7 quarts)

Cooling rack

Large saucepan (3 to 4 quarts)

12-cup and 24-cup muffin tins

8-inch and 13-by-9-inch metal baking pans

Rimmed baking sheet

KITCHEN BASICS

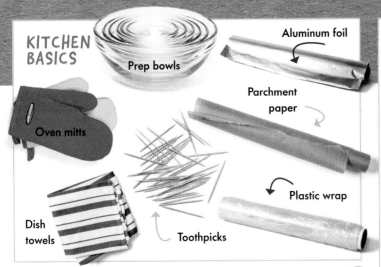

Prep bowls

Aluminum foil

Parchment paper

Oven mitts

Plastic wrap

Dish towels

Toothpicks

PREP TOOLS

Scale

Box grater

Ruler

Rasp grater

Dry measuring cups

Garlic press

Citrus juicer

Liquid measuring cup

Can opener

Measuring spoons

Vegetable peeler

COOKING & BAKING TOOLS

Instant-read thermometer

Rubber spatula

Whisk

Wooden spoon

Ladle

Tongs

Spatula

Pastry brush

Potato masher

Fine-mesh strainer

Icing spatula (offset)

Colander

Bench scraper

Rolling pin

chapter 1

everyday STAPLES

PEANUT BUTTER

Makes 1 cup | Total Time: 45 minutes

Make sure to use unsalted peanuts here; salted peanuts will make your peanut butter too salty! If you use raw (unroasted) peanuts, increase the toasting time in step 1 to 10 minutes.

PREPARE INGREDIENTS

- 2 cups dry-roasted unsalted peanuts
- 2 teaspoons honey
- ¼ teaspoon salt

GATHER COOKING EQUIPMENT

Rimmed baking sheet

Oven mitts

Cooling rack

Food processor

Rubber spatula

Jar with tight-fitting lid

"IT'S BETTER THAN STORE-BOUGHT PEANUT BUTTER!"

— ANNA, 10

START COOKING!

1 Adjust oven rack to middle position and heat oven to 375 degrees. Spread peanuts into even layer on rimmed baking sheet. Place baking sheet in oven. Toast peanuts until fragrant and shiny, about 5 minutes.

2 Use oven mitts to remove baking sheet from oven (ask an adult for help). Place baking sheet on cooling rack and let peanuts cool for 10 minutes.

3 Transfer peanuts to food processor, along with honey and salt. Lock lid into place. Turn on processor and process until peanuts break down and begin to clump together, about 2 minutes. Stop processor.

4 Remove lid. Use rubber spatula to scrape down sides of processor bowl. Lock lid back into place and process until smooth, 2 to 3 minutes. Stop processor.

5 Remove lid and carefully remove processor blade (ask an adult for help). Use rubber spatula to scrape peanut butter into jar with tight-fitting lid. (Peanut butter can be stored at room temperature or in refrigerator for up to 2 months.)

GOING NUTS FOR PEANUT BUTTER

Even though peanuts have been around for thousands of years, peanut butter didn't become popular until the 1920s. That's when inventors figured out how to guarantee that the peanut solids and the peanut oil wouldn't separate in the jar, making it easier to sell. Around the same time, presliced sandwich bread also became popular at the grocery store, and the peanut butter sandwich was born! This easy-to-make, high-protein sandwich became a lunch-box staple, and clever cooks added things such as jelly, bananas, or honey to make them extra-delicious. The peanut butter and jelly sandwich is now so popular, it's even been made by astronauts in space!

try it this way
CHUNKY PEANUT BUTTER

While peanuts are cooling in step 2, add an extra ¼ cup peanuts to food processor. Lock lid into place and pulse until peanuts are finely chopped, about 6 pulses. Remove lid and carefully remove processor blade (ask an adult for help). Transfer chopped peanuts to small bowl and set aside. In step 5, transfer peanut butter to bowl with chopped peanuts and stir to combine. Then transfer to jar with tight-fitting lid to store.

you can store it up to 2 months ... if you don't eat it all first!

CHOCOLATE HAZELNUT SPREAD

Makes 1½ cups | Total Time: 45 minutes

We prefer Dutch-processed cocoa powder in this recipe. You can substitute natural cocoa powder, but the spread will be slightly less intense and lighter in color.

PREPARE INGREDIENTS

- 2 cups skinned hazelnuts
- 1 cup confectioners' (powdered) sugar
- ⅓ cup Dutch-processed cocoa powder
- 2 tablespoons hazelnut, walnut, or vegetable oil
- 1 teaspoon vanilla extract
- ⅛ teaspoon salt

GATHER COOKING EQUIPMENT

Rimmed baking sheet

Oven mitts

Cooling rack

Food processor

Rubber spatula

Jar with tight-fitting lid

"IT WAS REALLY FUN USING A SCALE TO MEASURE THE HAZELNUTS!"
— JACK, 10

START COOKING!

1 Adjust oven rack to middle position and heat oven to 375 degrees. Spread hazelnuts into even layer on rimmed baking sheet. Place baking sheet in oven. Toast hazelnuts until fragrant and light brown, 6 to 8 minutes.

2 Use oven mitts to remove baking sheet from oven (ask an adult for help). Place baking sheet on cooling rack and let hazelnuts cool for 10 minutes.

3 Transfer hazelnuts to food processor. Lock lid into place. Turn on processor and process until hazelnuts form a smooth, loose paste, about 5 minutes, stopping frequently to scrape down sides of processor bowl with rubber spatula. Stop processor and remove lid.

4 Add confectioners' sugar, cocoa, oil, vanilla, and salt to processor. Lock lid back into place. Turn on processor and process until mixture begins to loosen slightly and becomes glossy, about 2 minutes. Stop processor, remove lid, and scrape down sides of processor bowl with rubber spatula as needed.

5 Carefully remove processor blade (ask an adult for help). Use rubber spatula to transfer chocolate hazelnut spread to jar with tight-fitting lid. (Chocolate hazelnut spread can be refrigerated for up to 1 month.)

HOWDY, HAZELNUTS!

This homemade spread is big on flavor and has a slightly chunkier texture than its supermarket cousin Nutella. Give it try—we promise you'll never go back to the store-bought version again! Hazelnut oil is available in fancy grocery stores and gourmet shops. It should be refrigerated once opened since it (and any nut oil) can go rancid more quickly than other cooking oils. We prefer using hazelnut oil here, but you could substitute walnut or even vegetable oil.

HOW TO SKIN HAZELNUTS

Hazelnut skins can make this spread taste bitter. Blanched and skinned hazelnuts are the easiest option for this recipe. If you can't find them, here's how to remove the skins at home.

1. Toast and cool hazelnuts as directed. Place cooled hazelnuts on clean dish towel. Fold towel to enclose nuts. Rub hazelnuts inside dish towel until skins peel off.

2. Open towel. Remove skinned hazelnuts, leaving bitter skins behind.

STRAWBERRY REFRIGERATOR JAM

Makes about 2 cups | Total Time: 1½ hours, plus 12 hours chilling time

PREPARE INGREDIENTS

1½ pounds strawberries

1 cup sugar

3 tablespoons lemon juice,
   squeezed from 1 lemon

GATHER COOKING EQUIPMENT

2 small plates

Cutting board

Chef's knife

Large saucepan

Potato masher

Rubber spatula

Spoon

Ladle

Jar with tight-fitting lid

" I LIKED SMASHING
THE STRAWBERRIES."
— ISABELLA, 9

START COOKING!

1 Place 2 small plates in freezer to chill. Use knife to hull strawberries (see photo, right). Cut each strawberry into quarters.

2 Transfer strawberries to large saucepan. Use potato masher to mash until fruit is mostly broken down. Add sugar and lemon juice and use rubber spatula to stir until combined.

3 Place saucepan over medium heat and bring to boil. Cook, stirring often with rubber spatula, until mixture is thickened, about 20 minutes. Turn off heat and slide saucepan to cool burner. Let cool for 2 minutes.

4 Remove 1 plate from freezer. Carefully spoon small amount of jam onto chilled plate (ask an adult for help—jam mixture will be VERY hot). Return plate to freezer for 2 minutes.

5 Remove plate from freezer and drag your finger through jam (see photos, page 33). If your finger leaves distinct trail that doesn't close up, jam is done! If jam is still runny, return saucepan to medium heat and cook jam for 2 to 3 minutes more, then repeat test with second chilled plate.

6 Let jam cool in saucepan for 15 minutes. Use ladle to transfer jam to jar with tight-fitting lid (ask an adult for help). Let jam cool completely, about 30 minutes. Place lid on jar.

7 Place jam in refrigerator until thickened and firm, 12 to 24 hours. Serve. (Jam can be refrigerated for up to 2 months.)

KEEP GOING →

HOW TO HULL STRAWBERRIES

The hull is the leafy green part of the strawberry. Use a knife to remove it as well as some of the whiteish berry right underneath the leaves (this part of the berry can be tough).

Place strawberry on its side and use knife to carefully cut off top with leafy green part.

MORE!
REFRIGERATOR JAM

JAMMING OUT

Have you ever wondered about the difference between jam and jelly? Wonder no more! Jam is made by cooking chopped or crushed fruit with sugar until it's spreadable but still has little pieces of fruit in it. Jelly, on the other hand, is made with fruit juice and sugar, so its texture is supersmooth, with no fruit pieces or bits. There are other kinds of fruit spreads, too, such as marmalade (made with orange peels), preserves (made with large pieces of fruit or whole berries in a sweet syrup), and fruit butter (made with fruit that's cooked for a long time and pureed to a thick, smooth texture).

try it this way
BLUEBERRY REFRIGERATOR JAM

Use 1 pound blueberries instead of strawberries. Do not mash in step 2. Reduce cooking time in step 3 to 10 minutes.

PEACH REFRIGERATOR JAM

Use 1 pound ripe peaches instead of strawberries. Pit peaches and chop into ½-inch pieces (no need to peel peaches). Reduce cooking time in step 3 to 15 minutes.

" I LIKED SMASHING THE STRAWBERRIES."
- EMELINE, 12

you can
still see
pieces
of fruit

RASPBERRY-CHOCOLATE JAM

Makes about 2½ cups | Total Time: 1 hour and 15 minutes, plus 12 hours chilling time

PREPARE INGREDIENTS

- 3¼ cups (1 pound) fresh or frozen raspberries (thawed if frozen)
- 1½ cups sugar
- 1½ teaspoons lemon juice, squeezed from ½ lemon
- ⅓ cup bittersweet or semisweet chocolate chips

GATHER COOKING EQUIPMENT

2 small plates

Large saucepan

Rubber spatula

Whisk

Spoon

Ladle

Jar with tight-fitting lid

> "I HAVE SEEN MY MOTHER MAKE JAM BUT HAVE NEVER MADE IT BY MYSELF. IT WAS FUN!" – JOSIE, 10

START COOKING!

1 Place 2 small plates in freezer to chill. Add raspberries, sugar, and lemon juice to large saucepan and use rubber spatula to stir until combined.

2 Place saucepan over medium heat and cook until juice begins to bubble at edges of saucepan, about 3 minutes. Continue to cook, stirring often with rubber spatula, until raspberries have broken down and released their juice, about 5 minutes.

3 Carefully add chocolate chips. Slowly whisk until completely melted, about 30 seconds (ask an adult for help—mixture will be VERY hot and, if you whisk too fast, it could splatter). Cook, carefully stirring often with rubber spatula, until mixture is thickened, about 5 minutes. Turn off heat and slide saucepan to cool burner. Let cool for 2 minutes.

4 Remove 1 plate from freezer. Carefully spoon small amount of jam onto chilled plate (ask an adult for help—jam mixture will be VERY hot). Return plate to freezer for 2 minutes.

5 Remove plate from freezer. Drag your finger through jam on plate (see photos, right). If your finger leaves distinct trail that doesn't close up, jam is done! If jam is still runny, return saucepan to medium heat and cook jam for 2 to 3 minutes more, then repeat test with second chilled plate.

6 Let jam cool in saucepan for 15 minutes. Use ladle to transfer jam to jar with tight-fitting lid (ask an adult for help). Let jam cool completely, about 30 minutes. Place lid on jar.

7 Place jam in refrigerator until thickened and firm, 12 to 24 hours. Serve. (Jam can be refrigerated for up to 2 months.)

use it this way

Spread this jam on toast or between slices of bread for a yummy sandwich. Or warm up this jam in the microwave and spoon it on top of ice cream or pound cake!

HOW TO DO THE PLATE TEST

As jam cooks, some of the water found in the fruit heats up, turns into steam, and evaporates. The longer you cook the jam, the more water evaporates and the thicker your jam will be. The plate test gives you a preview of the finished texture of your jam when it cools down. The freezer-chilled plate cools a small spoonful of hot jam, allowing you to run your finger through the jam. If the jam is runny, it still has too much water in it—keep cooking until the jam thickens up (or "sets") in your second plate test.

Jam is still too runny.

Finger leaves a clear trail—jam is done!

APPLESAUCE

Makes about 3½ cups | Total Time: 55 minutes

If you don't have a food mill, peel and core the apples before cooking and mash them at the end of step 4 with a potato masher. Your applesauce will be less pink and taste a little less like apples, but it will still be delicious!

PREPARE INGREDIENTS

2 pounds McIntosh apples (about 5 medium apples)

⅔ cup water

Pinch salt

Pinch ground cinnamon (optional)

Sugar (optional)

GATHER COOKING EQUIPMENT

Cutting board

Chef's knife

Large saucepan with lid

Oven mitts

Rubber spatula

Food mill

Large bowl

Ladle

1-teaspoon measuring spoon

Airtight storage container

"THE HOUSE SMELLED SO GOOD! AND EATING WARM APPLESAUCE WAS A REAL BIG TREAT THAT I NEED MORE OF!"
- MACEY, 11

START COOKING!

1 Cut apples into quarters on cutting board.

2 Place apples in large saucepan. Add water, salt, and cinnamon (if using). Cover and cook over medium heat until apples are soft and broken down, 20 to 25 minutes. During cooking, use oven mitts to remove lid and use rubber spatula to stir a few times.

3 Turn off heat and slide saucepan to cool burner. Use oven mitts to uncover and let apples cool for at least 15 minutes.

4 Set food mill over large bowl (see photos, right). Working in batches, use ladle to transfer apples to food mill basket. Crank apples through food mill into bowl. Discard skins and seeds left behind in food mill.

5 If you like, add a small amount of sugar to applesauce, 1 teaspoon at a time, and taste until applesauce has desired sweetness. Serve warm or at room temperature or transfer to airtight storage container. (Applesauce can be refrigerated for up to 1 week.)

(ALMOST) NO BAD APPLES

This applesauce works with just about any apple. Different types make different colors of applesauce—red apples make a pinker sauce, and green or yellow apples make a yellower sauce. We especially liked McIntosh, Jonagold, or Pink Lady apples in this recipe. The only apples we didn't like for this applesauce were Red and Golden Delicious—Red Delicious were too sweet, and Golden Delicious never fully broke down.

HOW TO USE A FOOD MILL

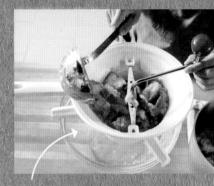

1. Set food mill over large bowl (ask an adult to show you how). Working in batches, use ladle to transfer apples to food mill basket.

2. Crank apples through food mill into bowl. Discard skins and seeds left behind in food mill.

APPLE A-PEEL

Apple skin is full of flavor, so keeping the peels on during cooking transfers apple flavor and a pretty pink color to the finished sauce. But the peels aren't that fun to eat. Enter: the food mill! This handy tool pushes the cooked apples through small holes, making the applesauce smooth and leaving the peels (and cores and seeds!) behind.

KETCHUP

Makes about 1½ cups | Total Time: 1½ hours, plus 12 hours chilling time

You can use cherry tomatoes instead of the grape tomatoes, but because they are juicier, you will need to cook them a little longer. In step 3, increase the cooking time to 12 to 15 minutes.

PREPARE INGREDIENTS

2¼ pounds grape tomatoes

1 garlic clove, peeled (see page 17)

½ cup red wine vinegar

½ cup packed dark brown sugar

2 teaspoons salt

½ teaspoon pepper

Pinch ground allspice

GATHER COOKING EQUIPMENT

12-inch nonstick skillet

Rubber spatula

Blender

Dish towel

Fine-mesh strainer

Medium bowl

Jar with tight-fitting lid

> **THE BEST PART WAS WATCHING THE TOMATOES POP. THE HARDEST WAS USING THE STRAINER."**
> **– BROOKE, 11**

START COOKING!

1 Add all ingredients to 12-inch nonstick skillet. Use rubber spatula to stir to combine.

2 Bring tomato mixture to simmer over medium-high heat. Reduce heat to medium and simmer, stirring occasionally and scraping bottom of skillet, about 20 minutes.

3 Reduce heat to low and continue to cook until almost all liquid has evaporated and rubber spatula leaves distinct trail when dragged across bottom of skillet (see photo, right), 5 to 10 minutes. Turn off heat. Let mixture cool for 15 minutes.

4 Ask an adult to carefully transfer tomatoes and liquid to blender jar. Place lid on top of blender and hold lid firmly in place with folded dish towel (see page 38). Turn on blender and process mixture until smooth, about 1 minute. Stop blender.

5 Set fine-mesh strainer over medium bowl. Pour tomato mixture into fine-mesh strainer (see photos, page 41). Use rubber spatula to stir and press on mixture to push liquid through strainer into bowl. Discard solids left in strainer.

6 Let ketchup cool to room temperature, about 30 minutes. Pour ketchup into jar with tight-fitting lid. Place in refrigerator until chilled and thickened, at least 12 hours. (Ketchup can be refrigerated for up to 1 month.)

KEEP GOING →

Cook tomato mixture until almost all liquid has evaporated and rubber spatula leaves distinct trail when dragged across bottom of skillet.

BLENDER SAFETY

When using the blender to puree a sauce or soup or make a smoothie, follow two simple rules:

1. Don't fill the blender jar more than two-thirds full.

2. Make sure to hold the lid securely in place with a folded dish towel. Then turn on the blender, keeping pressure on the towel so the lid stays in place.

This second rule is especially important when pureeing hot sauce or soup—the steam in the blender can loosen the lid, and hot liquid could shoot up in the air if you're not holding the lid in place. No one wants soup on the ceiling!

FRESH TOMATO KETCHUP

There's no denying it: Americans love ketchup. Ninety-seven percent of American households have ketchup in their kitchens, according to National Geographic. We've been slathering it on our burgers, french fries, grilled cheese sandwiches, scrambled eggs, and countless other foods for more than a century. For the most part, American families only use store-bought—but no longer! This recipe takes everything we love about this condiment and gets there with fresh tomatoes and traditional flavorings such as vinegar, garlic, brown sugar, and allspice. Homemade ketchup has even more tomato flavor than store-bought, making this ketchup extra-delicious!

"IT WAS THE BEST KETCHUP I HAVE EVER TASTED. I LOVED IT."
- KALLIE, 12

BARBECUE SAUCE

Makes 2 cups | Total Time: 40 minutes, plus cooling time

PREPARE INGREDIENTS

- 2 tablespoons vegetable oil
- 1 onion, peeled and chopped (see page 17)
- 2 garlic cloves, peeled and minced (see page 17)
- 1 teaspoon chili powder
- 1½ cups ketchup (store-bought or see page 36)
- ¼ cup molasses
- 3 tablespoons Worcestershire sauce
- 3 tablespoons cider vinegar
- 2 tablespoons Dijon mustard
- 1 teaspoon hot sauce (optional) (store-bought or see page 42)

GATHER COOKING EQUIPMENT

Large saucepan

Rubber spatula

Fine-mesh strainer

Medium bowl

Jar with tight-fitting lid

"MMM GOOD. I WAS EATING THE SAUCE WITH A SPOON."
— KAYLA, 9

START COOKING!

1 In large saucepan, heat oil over medium heat for 1 minute (oil should be hot but not smoking). Add onion and cook, stirring occasionally with rubber spatula, until onion is softened, about 5 minutes.

2 Stir in garlic and chili powder and cook for 1 minute. Add ketchup, molasses, Worcestershire, vinegar, mustard, and hot sauce (if using) and bring to simmer.

3 Reduce heat to low and cook, stirring occasionally, until flavors blend, about 5 minutes. Turn off heat. Let sauce cool slightly, 15 to 20 minutes.

4 Set fine-mesh strainer over medium bowl. Strain mixture through fine-mesh strainer, following photos, right (ask an adult for help—saucepan will be heavy). Discard solids left in strainer.

5 Let sauce cool to room temperature, about 30 minutes. Serve or transfer to jar with tight-fitting lid. (Barbecue sauce can be refrigerated for up to 1 week.)

GET SAUCY!

Where does barbecue sauce come from? One theory is that the earliest versions were first made in the Caribbean . . . but no one REALLY knows. Wherever it comes from, this centuries-old condiment is now an American staple. Today there are many different styles of barbecue sauce. One of the most popular styles is from Kansas City, Missouri, and is a thick, sweet, and tangy tomato-based sauce—which is exactly what inspired this recipe. How do YOU use barbecue sauce? On meat? Chicken? For dipping french fries? In our opinion, anything goes!

HOW TO STRAIN SAUCES

To make a smooth sauce or puree, we often use a fine-mesh strainer—a strainer made of material that looks like a window screen. The strainer will catch all the little bits that you don't want in your final sauce.

1. Set fine-mesh strainer over bowl. Pour or scrape sauce into strainer, asking an adult for help if working with a heavy pan.

2. Stir and press on mixture in strainer to push liquid through strainer into bowl. Discard solids in strainer.

41

HOT SAUCE

Makes about 1½ cups | Total Time: 1 hour and 15 minutes, plus 24 hours chilling time

We recommend wearing disposable gloves when preparing chiles because they can irritate your skin.

PREPARE INGREDIENTS

- 1 pound Fresno chiles, stemmed and seeded (see right)
- 1 red bell pepper, stemmed, seeded, and chopped (see page 44)
- 6 garlic cloves, peeled (see page 17)
- ½ cup water
- 6 tablespoons distilled white vinegar
- ¼ cup sugar
- 4 teaspoons salt
- 2 teaspoons fish sauce

GATHER COOKING EQUIPMENT

Blender

Dish towel

Large saucepan

Whisk

Rubber spatula

Fine-mesh strainer

Medium bowl

Jar with tight-fitting lid

"IT HAD JUST THE RIGHT AMOUNT OF SPICINESS! AWESOME!"
— ABBY, 12 & EVIE, 10

START COOKING!

1 Add Fresno chiles, bell pepper, garlic, water, and vinegar to blender jar. Place lid on top of blender and hold lid firmly in place with folded dish towel (see page 38). Turn on blender and process until smooth, 1 to 2 minutes. Stop blender.

2 Pour mixture into large saucepan. Whisk in sugar, salt, and fish sauce.

3 Bring mixture to boil over high heat. Reduce heat to medium-low and simmer, stirring occasionally with rubber spatula, until mixture is thickened, 25 to 30 minutes. Turn off heat and slide saucepan to cool burner. Let mixture cool for 15 minutes.

4 Use rubber spatula to scrape mixture into clean blender jar. Place lid on top of blender and hold lid firmly in place with folded dish towel. Turn on blender and process until smooth, 1 to 2 minutes. Stop blender.

5 Set fine-mesh strainer over medium bowl. Pour mixture into fine-mesh strainer (see photos, page 41). Use rubber spatula to stir and press on mixture to push liquid through strainer into bowl. Discard solids left in strainer.

6 Pour hot sauce into jar with tight-fitting lid. Place in refrigerator for at least 24 hours to let flavors develop. (Hot sauce can be refrigerated for up to 1 month.)

KEEP GOING →

HOW TO STEM AND SEED CHILES

Chiles contain a compound called capsaicin that makes them spicy. To make sure you do not get it on your skin or in your eyes, make sure to wear disposable gloves when touching chiles.

1. Hold chile firmly with 1 hand, with stem facing out. Use chef's knife to slice off top.

2. Use tip of teaspoon to scoop out seeds and ribs. If chile is too small, you can use spoon handle to scrape out seeds and stems. Discard seeds and stems.

HOW TO STEM, SEED, AND CHOP BELL PEPPERS

1. Slice off top and bottom of pepper with chef's knife. Remove seeds, stems, and ribs.

2. Slice down through side of pepper.

3. Press pepper so it lays flat on cutting board. Slice pepper lengthwise (the long way) into ½-inch-wide strips. Turn strips and cut crosswise (the short way) into ½-inch pieces.

CAN YOU TAKE THE HEAT?

Different types of chiles have different levels of spiciness. (Most of the heat in chiles actually lives in their seeds, which is why we remove them for this recipe.) Food scientists rate the spiciness of chiles on something called the Scoville Scale, which was invented in 1912 and is based on tasters' assessment of how much each chile sample would need to be diluted with sugar water before it no longer tasted hot. Mild Fresno peppers (like the ones in this recipe) are rated 2,500 to 10,000 Scoville heat units, while the REALLY spicy ghost pepper comes in at 800,000 to 1,000,000. Now that's one spicy pepper!

don't try it just yet... the flavors develop during refrigeration

SWEET-AND-SOUR SAUCE

Makes about 1½ cups | Total Time: 45 minutes, plus 1 hour chilling time

PREPARE INGREDIENTS

- 1 cup apple jelly
- ⅓ cup pineapple juice
- 4 teaspoons cornstarch
- 1 tablespoon low-sodium soy sauce
- 2 teaspoons distilled white vinegar
- 1 teaspoon Asian chili-garlic sauce
- ¼ teaspoon onion powder
- ¼ teaspoon paprika

GATHER COOKING EQUIPMENT

Large saucepan

Whisk

Rubber spatula

Jar with tight-fitting lid

"IT WAS THE PERFECT MIX OF SOUR AND SWEET AND I REALLY LIKED IT BECAUSE OF THAT." - SPENCER, 11

START COOKING!

1 In large saucepan, whisk all ingredients until well combined.

2 Bring mixture to simmer over medium heat. Cook, whisking occasionally, until mixture turns shiny and thickens slightly, about 3 minutes.

3 Turn off heat and slide saucepan to cool burner. Let sauce cool completely, about 30 minutes.

4 Use rubber spatula to scrape sauce into jar with tight-fitting lid. Place in refrigerator until chilled and thickened, about 1 hour. (Sweet-and-sour sauce can be refrigerated for up to 2 weeks.)

use it this way

You can use this sweet-and-sour sauce as a dip for chicken nuggets or french fries, stir it into a stir-fry, or toss it with cooked vegetables such as broccoli or green beans for an easy side dish.

SWEET AND SOUR (AND SALTY AND UMAMI!)

What is it about sweet-and-sour sauce that tastes SO good? It may have to do with your tongue . . . the tastebuds on your tongue and in your mouth can detect five different tastes in food: bitter, sweet, salty, sour, and umami (or savory). This sauce combines lots of those tastes, so there's lots of information for your tastebuds to send to your brain (and say "yum!"). This sauce gets sweetness from the apple jelly and pineapple juice, sourness from the vinegar, saltiness from the soy sauce, and umami from the chili-garlic sauce and onion powder.

MAYONNAISE

Makes 1 cup | Total Time: 15 minutes

PREPARE INGREDIENTS

- 1 large egg
- 1 tablespoon lemon juice, squeezed from ½ lemon
- 1 teaspoon distilled white vinegar
- ½ teaspoon Dijon mustard
- ½ teaspoon salt
- ¼ teaspoon sugar
- 1 cup vegetable oil

GATHER COOKING EQUIPMENT

Food processor

Liquid measuring cup

Rubber spatula

Jar with tight-fitting lid

"IT WAS EASY TO DO, BUT THE FOOD PROCESSOR IS REALLY NOISY."
— MORGAN, 7

START COOKING!

1 Add egg, lemon juice, vinegar, mustard, salt, and sugar to food processor. Lock lid into place. Turn on processor and process until ingredients are combined, about 10 seconds.

2 With processor running, VERY slowly drizzle oil through feed tube until mixture is thick, about 1 minute (see photo, right). Stop processor.

3 Remove lid and use rubber spatula to scrape down sides of processor bowl. Lock lid back into place. Process until smooth and creamy, about 30 seconds. Stop processor.

4 Remove lid and carefully remove processor blade (ask an adult for help). Use rubber spatula to transfer mayonnaise into jar with tight-fitting lid. Serve. (Mayonnaise can be refrigerated for up to 1 week.)

THE MAGIC OF EMULSIFICATION!

If you just casually stirred together all the ingredients of this recipe, you would end up with a broken, greasy mess. But if you add the oil VERY slowly to the food processor, your mayo will be creamy and smooth. What gives? It all comes down to the fact that oil and water don't like to mix. But (spoiler!) there is a way to get oil and water to play nicely. You have to turn them into an emulsion ("ih-MUHL-shun"). *Emulsion* is a science term for a combination of two liquids that don't usually mix, such as oil and water—or in this case, lemon juice and vinegar (the water) and vegetable oil. When you add the oil superslowly to the other ingredients while the food processor blade is whipping around, the oil breaks into teeny tiny droplets (as many as 30 billion droplets from 1 tablespoon of oil!) that then blend into the supercreamy mixture. Bonus: The egg yolk also contains something special called lecithin that helps it all stay together.

HOW TO ADD LIQUID TO A RUNNING FOOD PROCESSOR

While the processor is running, VERY slowly drizzle the oil down the feed tube that is part of the food processor lid. You want to go slow, just a little at a time. This helps turn the oil and other liquid ingredients into a creamy emulsion.

49

RANCH DRESSING

Makes 1 cup | Total Time: 15 minutes

PREPARE INGREDIENTS

- ⅔ cup mayonnaise (store-bought or see page 48)
- ⅓ cup buttermilk
- 2 tablespoons minced fresh cilantro (see page 16)
- 2 teaspoons white wine vinegar
- ½ teaspoon onion powder
- ½ teaspoon garlic powder
- ¼ teaspoon dried dill weed
- ⅛ teaspoon salt
- ⅛ teaspoon pepper

GATHER COOKING EQUIPMENT

Medium bowl

Whisk

Jar with tight-fitting lid

"TASTES EVEN BETTER THAN THE RANCH DRESSING AT MY FAVORITE RESTAURANT. I RENAMED THIS AWESOME SAUCE." – ALYSSA, 13

START COOKING!

In medium bowl, combine all ingredients and whisk until smooth. Transfer to jar with tight-fitting lid. Serve. (Ranch dressing can be refrigerated for up to 4 days.)

THE ORIGINS OF RANCH

When Kenneth Henson was 29 years old and working in Alaska as a plumbing contractor, he developed a buttermilk-based salad dressing one night when making dinner. Everyone loved it so much that when Henson moved to California in the early 1950s and bought a dude ranch (that he named Hidden Valley), he started to sell his famous salad dressing. (You've probably seen it on the supermarket shelves!) He also developed the famous brand of "ranch" seasoning packets Americans grew to love, which led to ranch-flavored EVERYTHING!

BALSAMIC VINAIGRETTE

Makes about 1 cup | Total Time: 10 minutes

Make sure to use a jar that has some extra room in it after adding the ingredients—you want the liquid to be able to shake back and forth inside to get the oil and vinegar to mix. A pint-size jar works well.

PREPARE INGREDIENTS

- 1 tablespoon mayonnaise
- 1 tablespoon Dijon mustard
- 1 teaspoon maple syrup
- ½ teaspoon salt
- ¼ cup balsamic vinegar
- ¼ cup plus ¼ cup extra-virgin olive oil, measured separately
- ¼ cup vegetable oil

GATHER COOKING EQUIPMENT

Jar with tight-fitting lid

Fork

"IT WAS TANGY BUT SWEET, WHICH MADE IT DELICIOUS WITH SALAD."
– NATALIE, 11

START COOKING!

1 Add mayonnaise, mustard, maple syrup, and salt to jar with tight-fitting lid. Use fork to stir until mixture is well combined and smooth.

2 Add vinegar and cover jar with lid to seal. Shake until smooth (see photo, below), about 10 seconds.

3 Remove lid. Add ¼ cup olive oil and re-cover jar with lid. Shake until combined, about 10 seconds. Add remaining ¼ cup olive oil and repeat shaking.

4 Add vegetable oil and shake until dressing is smooth and slightly thickened and has no extra oil floating on surface. Serve. (Dressing can be refrigerated for up to 1 week. Shake briefly before using.)

READY, SET, EMULSIFY!

A vinaigrette is an example of an emulsion, a mixture of two liquids that usually don't like to mix. In this case, those two liquids are oil and vinegar. (Another example of an emulsion is mayonnaise, see page 48.) Usually, when mixed together, oil and vinegar push apart and separate out into two different layers. By adding a special ingredient called an emulsifier and mixing vigorously, you can get those layers to break apart into tiny droplets and stick together into a smooth dressing. In this recipe, we add mustard and mayonnaise as the emulsifiers and shake everything up in a jar in stages until a smooth, creamy vinaigrette forms. By using some vegetable oil in addition to olive oil, this dressing will also stay emulsified in the fridge for up to a week! Time to get shaking.

BREAD AND BUTTER PICKLE CHIPS

Makes about 2 cups | Total Time: 2 hours, plus 2 hours chilling time

Make sure to buy small pickling cucumbers (called Kirby cucumbers) for this recipe.

PREPARE INGREDIENTS

- 1 pound pickling (Kirby) cucumbers, trimmed and sliced crosswise into ⅛-inch-thick circles (see photo, right)
- ½ onion, peeled and sliced thin (see page 57)
- 1 tablespoon kosher salt
- 1 cup cider vinegar
- ¾ cup sugar
- ½ teaspoon yellow mustard seeds
- ¼ teaspoon celery seeds
- ⅛ teaspoon ground turmeric

GATHER COOKING EQUIPMENT

Colander

Large bowl

Wooden spoon

Large saucepan with lid

Oven mitts

Slotted spoon

Jar with tight-fitting lid

Ladle

"IT WAS EASY TO CHOP THE CUCUMBERS BUT SLIGHTLY HARD TO MAKE THE ONIONS THIN."
— MARISA, 10

START COOKING!

1 Place colander in large bowl. Add cucumbers and onion to colander and sprinkle with salt. Use wooden spoon to toss until combined. Let sit for 1 hour. Discard drained liquid.

2 In large saucepan, combine vinegar, sugar, mustard seeds, celery seeds, and turmeric. Use wooden spoon to combine. Bring to boil over high heat.

3 Reduce heat to low and ask an adult to carefully add drained cucumbers and onion to saucepan (vinegar mixture will be VERY hot). Press with wooden spoon to submerge vegetables in liquid. Cover and cook until cucumbers turn dullish olive brown, 5 to 7 minutes. Turn off heat.

4 Use oven mitts to remove lid. Let cool for 15 minutes. Use slotted spoon to carefully transfer pickles to jar with tight-fitting lid. Use ladle to cover pickles with brine (ask an adult for help). Let pickles cool completely, about 30 minutes.

5 Cover jar with lid. Place in refrigerator until chilled, at least 2 hours. (Pickles can be refrigerated for up to 6 weeks.)

HOW TO SLICE CUCUMBERS

Trim ends off cucumber. Slice cucumber crosswise into ⅛-inch-thick circles.

COOL AS A CUCUMBER

There are many varieties of cucumbers in all sorts of shapes, sizes, and colors. The most common cucumber you'll find at the grocery store is the American cucumber, which has a thick green skin and lots of big seeds. English cucumbers are long and slim, have thin skins and small seeds, and usually come wrapped in plastic. Persian cucumbers are basically mini versions of English cucumbers and are great for snacking. Kirby cucumbers (the kind we call for in this recipe) are small and squat and are great for making pickles.

Persian Cucumber

Kirby Cucumber

English Cucumber

American Cucumber

PICKLED RED ONIONS

Makes about 1 cup | Total Time: 35 minutes

PREPARE INGREDIENTS

- 1 small red onion
- 1 cup white wine vinegar
- 2 tablespoons lime juice, squeezed from 1 lime
- 1 tablespoon sugar
- 1 teaspoon salt

GATHER COOKING EQUIPMENT

Cutting board

Chef's knife

Medium bowl

Small saucepan

Fine-mesh strainer

Jar with tight-fitting lid

IT WAS EASY—THEY WERE GREAT ON FISH TACOS!"

– CAROLINE, 12

START COOKING!

1 Slice onion into thin strips following photos, right. Place sliced onion in medium bowl.

2 In small saucepan, combine vinegar, lime juice, sugar, and salt. Bring to boil over high heat. Turn off heat.

3 Carefully pour vinegar mixture over onion (ask an adult for help—mixture will be VERY hot). Let mixture cool completely, about 30 minutes.

4 When mixture is cool, drain onions in fine-mesh strainer over sink, discarding liquid. Transfer to jar with tight-fitting lid. Serve. (Pickled onions can be refrigerated for up to 4 days.)

THE POWER OF A BRINE!

A 30-minute bath in this salty-sweet brine (made with vinegar, lime juice, sugar, and salt) is all it takes to transform an everyday sliced onion into tangy, crunchy pickles—the perfect topping for tacos, burgers, or sandwiches. All kinds of thinly sliced vegetables can be pickled using this same method, including cucumbers, carrots, fennel, and radishes.

HOW TO SLICE ONIONS

1. Slice onion in half through root end, then use your fingers to remove peel.

2. Place onion halves flat side down on cutting board. Trim off ends and discard. Then slice onion vertically into thin strips, following grain (long stripes on onion).

BASIL PESTO

Makes about ¾ cup | Total Time: 30 minutes

PREPARE INGREDIENTS

- ¼ cup pine nuts
- 2 cups fresh basil leaves
- ½ cup extra-virgin olive oil
- ¼ cup grated Parmesan cheese (½ ounce)
- 1 garlic clove, peeled (see page 17)
- ½ teaspoon salt

GATHER COOKING EQUIPMENT

10-inch skillet

Rubber spatula

Food processor

Airtight storage container

"YUMMY AND COLORFUL AND SMELLS WONDERFUL."

- KATIE, 11

START COOKING!

1 Add pine nuts to 10-inch skillet and toast, following photo, right.

2 Carefully transfer pine nuts to food processor (ask an adult for help) and let pine nuts cool for 10 minutes.

3 Add basil, oil, Parmesan, garlic, and salt to food processor. Lock lid into place. Turn on processor and process for 30 seconds. Stop processor, remove lid, and use rubber spatula to scrape down sides of processor bowl.

4 Lock lid back into place. Turn on processor and process until mixture is smooth, about 30 seconds. Stop processor, remove lid, and carefully remove processor blade (ask an adult for help).

5 Use rubber spatula to scrape pesto into airtight storage container. Serve. (Pesto can be covered with 1 tablespoon oil and refrigerated for up to 4 days.)

HOW TO TOAST NUTS

Toasting nuts (and seeds) maximizes their flavor, so whether you are using them in pesto or sprinkling them over a salad, it pays to spend a few minutes toasting nuts. The best way to toast a small amount of nuts (less than 1 cup) is in a dry skillet on the stovetop. Make sure to watch the nuts closely because they can go from golden to burnt VERY quickly!

Place nuts in 10-inch skillet. Toast nuts over low heat, stirring often with rubber spatula, until lightly browned and fragrant, 6 to 8 minutes. Turn off heat.

PESTO IS THE BESTO!

The word pesto comes from the Italian word pestare, which means "to pound." Pesto is traditionally made in a mortar and pestle. Basil leaves, pine nuts, and garlic are placed in the mortar (a heavy bowl) and then crushed and mashed together into a paste with the pestle (a short handheld object with a rounded bottom). A food processor produces pesto in seconds—no pounding needed!

FRESH TOMATO SALSA

Makes about 2 cups | Total Time: 55 minutes

We recommend wearing disposable gloves when preparing chiles because they can irritate your skin.

PREPARE INGREDIENTS

- 1 pound ripe plum tomatoes (4 to 6 tomatoes)
- 1 teaspoon salt
- ¼ cup fresh cilantro leaves
- ½ jalapeño chile, seeded and chopped (see page 43)
- 1 small shallot, peeled and chopped (see page 17)
- 2 teaspoons lime juice, squeezed from 1 lime
- ¼ teaspoon chili powder

GATHER COOKING EQUIPMENT

Cutting board

Paring knife

Colander

Rubber spatula

1-cup dry measuring cup

Food processor

Airtight storage container

> " **IT WAS DELICIOUS, ESPECIALLY ON NACHOS."**
> **– DANIEL, 11**

START COOKING!

1 Cut each tomato following photos, right.

2 Place colander in sink. Transfer tomatoes to colander and sprinkle with salt. Use rubber spatula to gently stir to combine. Let tomatoes drain for 30 minutes.

3 When tomatoes are ready, tip and shake colander to drain any remaining liquid. Use 1-cup dry measuring cup to transfer 1 cup tomatoes to food processor and lock lid into place. Turn on processor and process until tomatoes are broken down, about 15 seconds. Stop processor.

4 Remove lid and add cilantro, jalapeño, shallot, lime juice, chili powder, and remaining tomatoes to food processor. Lock lid back into place. Hold down pulse button for 1 second, then release. Repeat until mixture is chopped but not totally broken down, about five 1-second pulses.

5 Remove lid and carefully remove processor blade (ask an adult for help). Use rubber spatula to scrape salsa into airtight storage container. Serve. (Salsa can be refrigerated for up to 2 days.)

SECRETS TO SUCCESSFUL SALSA

In Spanish, salsa means "sauce," but in English, it usually refers to a spicy dip made from chopped tomatoes. You can put all kinds of ingredients into a salsa, but this one uses the classic flavors of Mexican pico de gallo, including onion, chile, cilantro, and lime. Just chopping up these ingredients and mixing them together can make your salsa more like a salad than a dip. Plus, tomatoes have a lot of juice that can make your salsa watery. To solve these problems, we sprinkle the tomatoes with salt to draw out their extra juice, and then blend some of the tomatoes into a smooth sauce to bring all the other ingredients together. This salsa is fresh and dippable!

HOW TO CHOP TOMATOES

1. Use paring knife to cut tomato in half from top to bottom (through stem end).

2. Place each half flat side down. Use tip of knife to cut out core from each half and discard.

3. Cut each tomato half into quarters (4 pieces).

ROASTED RED PEPPER HUMMUS

Makes about 1½ cups | Total Time: 20 minutes

PREPARE INGREDIENTS

- 2 tablespoons water
- 2 tablespoons lemon juice, squeezed from 1 lemon
- 2 tablespoons tahini (stirred well before measuring)
- 2 tablespoons extra-virgin olive oil
- 1 (15-ounce) can chickpeas
- ¼ cup jarred roasted red peppers, patted dry with paper towels
- 1 garlic clove, peeled (see page 17)
- ½ teaspoon salt

GATHER COOKING EQUIPMENT

Liquid measuring cup

Spoon

Colander

Can opener

Food processor

Rubber spatula

Airtight storage container

“IT WAS ABSOLUTELY DELICIOUS!
WE HAVE TO MAKE THIS AGAIN!"
- GRACE, 13 & EMMA, 11

START COOKING!

1 In liquid measuring cup, use spoon to stir together water, lemon juice, tahini, and oil.

2 Set colander in sink. Open can of chickpeas and pour into colander. Rinse chickpeas with cold water and shake colander to drain well.

3 Transfer chickpeas to food processor. Add red peppers, garlic, and salt to processor and lock lid into place. Turn on processor and process for 10 seconds.

4 Stop processor, remove lid, and scrape down sides of bowl with rubber spatula. Lock lid back into place. Turn on processor and process until mixture is coarsely ground, about 5 seconds.

5 With processor running, slowly pour water mixture through feed tube until mixture is smooth, about 1 minute (see photo, page 49).

6 Stop processor, remove lid, and carefully remove processor blade (ask an adult for help). Use rubber spatula to scrape hummus into airtight storage container. Serve. (Hummus can be refrigerated for up to 5 days. Before serving, stir in 1 tablespoon warm water to loosen hummus.)

TAHINI TRAIL MAP

Tahini is a creamy ground sesame paste that helps give hummus its nutty flavor and smooth texture. It is a key ingredient in Middle Eastern food, but did you know that the sesame seed plant (called *Sesamum indicum*) is actually native to Africa? Today, teeny tiny sesame seeds (there are 7,500 to 9,000 seeds per ounce!) are mostly grown in India, China, Mexico, and Sudan.

try it this way
LEMONY HERB HUMMUS

Increase water to ¼ cup. Use ¼ cup fresh mint or cilantro leaves instead of roasted red peppers. Add ½ teaspoon grated lemon zest (see page 16) to food processor along with garlic in step 3.

BUTTER

Makes about ¾ cup
Total Time: 20 minutes, plus chilling time

PREPARE INGREDIENTS

2 cups heavy cream

¼ teaspoon salt (optional)

GATHER COOKING EQUIPMENT

Food processor

Fine-mesh strainer

2 bowls (1 large, 1 medium)

Airtight storage container

> **"MY FAMILY WAS WATCHING ME SQUEEZE THE BUTTER AND THEY ALL THOUGHT IT WAS VERY FUNNY."**
> **- MACKENZIE, 12**

START COOKING!

1 Pour cream into food processor and lock lid into place. Turn on processor and process until cream whips and turns into lumpy, liquid-y butter mixture, 2 to 4 minutes (see photo 1, page 66). Stop processor, remove lid, and carefully remove processor blade (ask an adult for help).

2 Place fine-mesh strainer over large bowl. Pour mixture from processor into strainer and let liquid drain away from butter lumps, about 2 minutes (see photo 2, page 66).

3 Knead butter, following photos 3 and 4, page 66.

4 Transfer butter to medium bowl and discard liquid in large bowl. Sprinkle salt (if using) over butter mixture. Use your hands to knead until combined.

5 Transfer butter to airtight storage container. Place in refrigerator until firm and chilled, about 30 minutes. Serve. (Butter can be refrigerated for up to 2 weeks.)

KEEP GOING →

HOW DOES CREAM BECOME BUTTER?

Cream has a bunch of (yummy!) milk fat particles swimming around in a mostly water base. Butter, on the other hand, is mostly milk fat particles stuck together in a solid mass. So how do we get the milk fat particles out of the cream? By churning cream (or processing it in the food processor), we beat air into it, which causes the fat particles to slam against each other and stick. This continues to happen, like a snowball getting bigger and bigger as it rolls, until almost all the fat in the cream is stuck together. Then, we get rid of the watery stuff left behind in the bowl and knead the butter mixture together with our hands to squeeze out extra water that's still hanging out between the fat particles. After joining the fat particles together and removing extra water, we have a substance that's more fat than water—and it happens to be delicious butter!

HOW TO MAKE AND KNEAD BUTTER

1. Turn on processor and process until cream whips and turns into lumpy, liquid-y butter mixture, 2 to 4 minutes.

2. Pour mixture into fine-mesh strainer and let drain for 2 minutes.

3. Use your hands to press butter lumps together to form ball.

4. Use your hands to knead butter ball, squeezing out extra liquid. Continue to knead until very little liquid comes out when butter is squeezed, about 2 minutes.

process until cream whips and separates

"NO ONE IN MY FAMILY HAS EVER HAD HOMEMADE BUTTER BEFORE, SO THAT MADE IT EXCITING. IT WAS CREAMY AND DELICIOUS!"
— HANNAH, 13

RICOTTA CHEESE

Makes about 2 cups | Total Time: 1 hour, plus 1½ hours chilling time

Make sure to use pasteurized milk here. If you use any other kind, the recipe won't work! Cheesecloth is a woven cotton fabric with lots of little holes in it. It can usually be found in the cookware or baking section of the grocery store.

PREPARE INGREDIENTS

- 8 cups pasteurized (not ultra-pasteurized or UHT) whole milk
- 1 teaspoon salt
- ¼ cup distilled white vinegar, plus extra as needed

GATHER COOKING EQUIPMENT

Cheesecloth

Colander

Large bowl

Large saucepan

Rubber spatula

Instant-read thermometer

Airtight storage container

"WHO KNEW MAKING RICOTTA CHEESE WAS SOOOO EASY?! AND IT TASTED DELICIOUS!!"
— VICTORIA, 13

START COOKING!

1 Lay triple layer of cheesecloth inside colander, with extra cheesecloth hanging over edge of colander. Place cheesecloth-lined colander in sink. Place large bowl next to sink.

2 In large saucepan, combine milk and salt. Place saucepan over medium-high heat and cook, stirring often with rubber spatula, until milk registers 185 degrees on instant-read thermometer, 12 to 15 minutes.

3 Turn off heat and slide saucepan to cool burner. Slowly pour in vinegar and use rubber spatula to stir until milk solids clump together, about 15 seconds. Let sit, without stirring, until mixture fully separates into solid curds on top and watery, yellowish whey (liquid) underneath, about 10 minutes (see photo, right).

4 Carefully pour mixture into cheesecloth-lined colander in sink (ask an adult for help—saucepan will be heavy and mixture will be HOT!). Let sit, without stirring, until whey has mostly drained away but cheese is still wet, about 1 minute.

5 Working quickly, strain ricotta and transfer to bowl, following photos, page 70. Let ricotta cool completely, about 30 minutes.

6 Transfer ricotta to airtight storage container. Place in refrigerator until chilled, about 1½ hours. (Ricotta can be refrigerated for up to 5 days.) Stir ricotta before serving.

KEEP GOING →

CURDS AND WHEY

Use a rubber spatula to gently pull the milk solids (called curds) away from the edge of the saucepan to see if they have clumped together and if the liquid left behind (called whey) is mostly clear. If the whey still looks like milk instead of a mostly clear liquid, stir in 1 more tablespoon of vinegar and let the mixture sit for 2 to 3 more minutes until the curds separate.

use it this way

You can use ricotta cheese in sweet and savory dishes. One of our favorite options? Spreading it on warm, crunchy toast. For a sweet version, try topping your toast with 1 to 2 tablespoons of ricotta, your favorite berries, and a drizzle of honey. Or go savory: Top your ricotta toast with halved cherry tomatoes, fresh basil, salt, pepper, and extra-virgin olive oil. Ricotta is also delicious dolloped on pasta or pizza right before you serve it.

RICOTTA CHEESE

HOW TO STRAIN RICOTTA

Some whey (liquid) may continue to drain out of the cheese as you transfer it to the bowl, but that's OK! Try to keep as much whey as you can with the cheese so that the ricotta turns out nice and creamy.

1. Working quickly, gather edges of cheesecloth into bundle and transfer cheese (inside cloth) to large bowl next to sink.

2. Slide cheesecloth out from under cheese (leaving cheese in bowl) and discard cheesecloth.

3. Use rubber spatula to break up large cheese curds.

NO WHEY!

A popular nursery rhyme begins with "Little Miss Muffet sat on her tuffet, eating her curds and whey." But what are curds and whey? They're two products of cheese making! Cheese is made by adding acid (such as vinegar or lemon juice) or rennet (an enzyme that can come from animals or plants) to milk. When you add acid to milk, it causes the proteins in the milk to link up together and clump tightly. This process is called coagulation. The solid lumps held together by these proteins are the curds, and the leftover liquid is the whey. Maybe Little Miss Muffet was eating ricotta on her tuffet!

AMERICAN CHEESE

Makes 1 pound | Total Time: 35 minutes, plus 3 hours chilling time

We prefer to use whole milk powder for this recipe. You can substitute nonfat milk powder, but your cheese will be softer. Make sure to use the small holes on the box grater to shred the Colby cheese so that it melts quickly.

PREPARE INGREDIENTS

- 1 tablespoon water
- 1½ teaspoons unflavored gelatin
- 3 cups finely shredded Colby cheese (12 ounces) (see page 15)
- 1 tablespoon whole milk powder
- ½ teaspoon salt
- ⅛ teaspoon cream of tartar
- ½ cup plus 2 tablespoons (5 ounces) whole milk

GATHER COOKING EQUIPMENT

5-by-4-inch disposable aluminum loaf pan

Plastic wrap

Small bowl

Food processor

Liquid measuring cup

Oven mitts

Spoon

Rubber spatula

" I LOVED THE WAY THE CHEESE TASTED AND FELT IN MY MOUTH."
- MARISA, 10

START COOKING!

1 Line 5-by-4-inch disposable aluminum loaf pan with plastic wrap, allowing excess to hang over sides.

2 Pour water into small bowl. Sprinkle gelatin over water and let sit until gelatin softens, about 5 minutes.

3 Add Colby, milk powder, salt, and cream of tartar to food processor and lock lid into place. Hold down pulse button for 1 second, then release. Repeat until ingredients are combined, about three 1-second pulses.

4 In liquid measuring cup, heat milk in microwave until beginning to bubble around edges, about 2 minutes. Use oven mitts to remove from microwave (ask an adult for help—milk will be VERY hot!). Use spoon to carefully scrape softened gelatin into measuring cup and stir until gelatin is dissolved.

5 With processor running, slowly pour warm milk mixture through feed tube until cheese mixture is smooth, about 1 minute (see photo, page 49). Stop processor, remove lid, and carefully remove processor blade (ask an adult for help).

6 Working quickly, use rubber spatula to scrape cheese into plastic-lined loaf pan. Pack tightly and cover, following photos, right.

7 Place loaf pan in refrigerator and chill for at least 3 hours to set. Serve. (American cheese can be refrigerated for up to 1 month.)

HOW TO SHAPE AMERICAN CHEESE

1. Working quickly, use rubber spatula to scrape cheese into plastic-lined loaf pan. Use rubber spatula to pack cheese firmly into loaf pan to remove any air pockets, then smooth top.

2. Fold overhanging plastic tightly over top of cheese and press against surface of cheese.

use it this way

Slice this cheese to make a grilled cheese sandwich, cut it up and use it to make creamy macaroni and cheese, or melt it and mix it with salsa for a creamy queso dip!

EVERYTHING BAGEL SEASONING

Makes ⅓ cup | Total Time: 15 minutes

PREPARE INGREDIENTS

- 2 tablespoons sesame seeds
- 2 teaspoons caraway seeds (optional)
- 1 tablespoon poppy seeds
- 1 tablespoon dried minced onion
- 1 tablespoon dried minced garlic
- 2 teaspoons kosher salt

GATHER COOKING EQUIPMENT

8-inch skillet

Rubber spatula

Small bowl

Small jar with tight-fitting lid

"IT WAS FUN AND TASTES AMAZING. I TRIED WITH AND WITHOUT CARAWAY SEEDS. WITH CARAWAY WAS MY FAVORITE." — LILLIAN, 10

START COOKING!

1 Add sesame seeds and caraway seeds (if using) to 8-inch skillet. Toast over medium-low heat, stirring often with rubber spatula, until fragrant and sesame seeds turn golden brown, 3 to 5 minutes. Turn off heat. Transfer seeds to small bowl and let cool to room temperature, about 10 minutes.

2 Add poppy seeds, dried minced onion, dried minced garlic, salt, and toasted seeds to small jar with tight-fitting lid. Cover jar with lid to seal and shake until combined. (Everything bagel seasoning can be stored at room temperature for up to 1 month.)

use it this way

Sprinkle on a plain bagel with cream cheese, over potato salad or hard-cooked eggs, or on vegetable dips.

HAVING IT ALL

Bagels come in lots of different flavors with all sorts of toppings, but "everything" is one of the most popular flavors in the United States. It's hard to know for sure who invented it, but one story goes that a teenager working at a bagel shop in Queens, New York, was cleaning out the oven at closing time and swept together all the toppings that had fallen off other bagels earlier in the day. He gave the combo of toasted seeds, garlic and onion bits, and salt to the baker and asked him to try to make a bagel with it and call it "everything." The flavor took off with customers and has become one of the most iconic bagel flavors of all time.

PUMPKIN SPICE MIX

Makes ⅓ cup | Total Time: 5 minutes

You can store your pumpkin spice mix in a clean, dry salt shaker—this way it's ready for you to sprinkle over your favorite foods!

PREPARE INGREDIENTS

- 2 tablespoons sugar
- 4 teaspoons ground cinnamon
- 1 teaspoon ground ginger
- ½ teaspoon ground nutmeg
- ½ teaspoon ground allspice

GATHER COOKING EQUIPMENT

Small jar with tight-fitting lid

EASY, PEASY, LEMON SQUEEZY. I LIKED THE SUGGESTIONS ABOUT HOW TO USE IT." – REX, 12

START COOKING!

Place all ingredients in jar with tight-fitting lid. Cover jar with lid to seal and shake until combined. (Pumpkin spice mix can be stored at room temperature for up to 1 month.)

try it this way

PUMPKIN SPICE BUTTER

Spread this butter on warm waffles, pancakes, toast, or rolls.
   In medium bowl, use rubber spatula to stir 6 tablespoons softened unsalted butter and 4 teaspoons pumpkin spice mix until well combined.

PUMPKIN SPICE HOT APPLE CIDER

A warm mug of this apple cider is a treat on a chilly fall day.
   Combine 1 cup apple cider and 1½ teaspoons pumpkin spice mix in liquid measuring cup. Heat in microwave until hot and steaming, about 2 minutes. Use oven mitts to carefully remove measuring cup from microwave (ask an adult for help). Whisk well to combine. Pour hot cider into mug. Serve.

PUMPKIN SPICE CREAM CHEESE

Spread this flavored cream cheese on bagels or toast—it's great on cinnamon swirl bread!
   In medium bowl, use rubber spatula to stir ½ cup softened cream cheese and 1 tablespoon pumpkin spice mix until well combined.

BUT WHERE'S THE PUMPKIN?

Did you ever wonder how "pumpkin spice" flavoring got its name, especially since it doesn't contain any . . . pumpkin? The flavor of "pumpkin spice" is a sweeter version of the spices you often find in—surprise!—pumpkin pie: cinnamon, nutmeg, ginger, allspice, and sometimes cloves. Pumpkin itself doesn't have a very strong flavor. That's why pumpkin pie tastes mostly like this sweet spice mix.

SNACKS

BAGEL CHIPS

Makes about 30 chips | Total Time: 50 minutes, plus cooling time

PREPARE INGREDIENTS

- 2 whole (unsliced) plain bagels
- 2 tablespoons extra-virgin olive oil
- ½ teaspoon kosher salt

GATHER COOKING EQUIPMENT

Cutting board

Chef's knife

Large bowl

Rimmed baking sheet

Oven mitts

Cooling rack

"MY FAVORITE PART WAS MIXING THE CHIPS WITH MY HANDS. IT FELT REALLY WEIRD."
- MALYCIA, 12

START COOKING!

1 Adjust oven rack to upper-middle position and heat oven to 275 degrees.

2 Place bagels flat side down on cutting board. Use knife to slice each bagel following photo, right; ask an adult for help.

3 Transfer bagel slices to large bowl. Drizzle oil over bagel slices and sprinkle with salt. Use your hands to toss until slices are evenly coated.

4 Transfer bagel slices to rimmed baking sheet and spread slices into single layer. Place baking sheet in oven. Bake until bagel chips are light golden brown, 30 to 35 minutes.

5 Use oven mitts to remove baking sheet from oven (ask an adult for help). Place baking sheet on cooling rack and let bagel chips cool completely on baking sheet, about 30 minutes. Serve. (Bagel chips can be stored at room temperature in airtight container for up to 5 days.)

FLAVORED CREAM CHEESE DIP

You can eat your bagel chips with any dip you like, but we especially like eating them with flavored cream cheese dip.

To make flavored cream cheese dip

In medium bowl, combine 4 ounces softened cream cheese and 3 tablespoons milk. Use fork to mash mixture until combined, then whisk mixture until smooth, about 1 minute. Add any one of the following ingredients to flavor your dip!

1   tablespoon minced scallion greens

1   tablespoon minced chives

1   tablespoon Everything Bagel Seasoning (see page 74)

1   teaspoon honey

HOW TO SLICE BAGEL CHIPS

Here is the best (and safest!) way to slice bagels for bagel chips. You'll end up with some long ovals and some smaller circles, all of which are great to use for dipping.

Place bagels flat side down on cutting board. Slice each bagel crosswise into ¼-inch-thick slices (ask an adult for help).

try it this way
GARLIC BAGEL CHIPS

Add 1 teaspoon granulated garlic to bowl along with oil and salt in step 3.

PARMESAN BAGEL CHIPS

Add ½ cup grated Parmesan cheese to bowl along with oil and salt in step 3.

PITA CHIPS

Makes 32 chips | Total Time: 35 minutes, plus cooling time

You can use whole-wheat pita bread, if you like. You can also substitute vegetable oil or melted butter for the olive oil.

PREPARE INGREDIENTS

- 2 (8-inch) pita breads
- ¼ cup extra-virgin olive oil
- ½ teaspoon kosher salt

GATHER COOKING EQUIPMENT

Kitchen shears

Pastry brush

Cutting board

Chef's knife

Rimmed baking sheet

Oven mitts

Cooling rack

"CRUNCHY AND SALTY! DELICIOUS!"
— ZERALINA, 9

START COOKING!

1 Adjust oven rack to middle position and heat oven to 325 degrees.

2 Use kitchen shears to cut around edge of each pita to separate into 2 thin rounds.

3 Working with 1 pita round at a time, use pastry brush to brush rough side generously with oil. Sprinkle evenly with salt.

4 Stack pita rounds and place on cutting board. Use chef's knife to cut pita stack into 8 equal wedges following photos, right.

5 Transfer pita wedges to rimmed baking sheet and spread into single layer, oiled side up. Place baking sheet in oven. Bake until wedges are golden brown and crisp, 15 to 18 minutes.

6 Use oven mitts to remove baking sheet from oven (ask an adult for help). Place baking sheet on cooling rack and let pita chips cool completely on baking sheet, about 30 minutes. Serve. (Pita chips can be stored at room temperature in airtight container for up to 4 days.)

try it this way
BUTTERMILK-RANCH PITA CHIPS

Use 1 tablespoon packaged buttermilk-ranch seasoning powder instead of salt.

CHILI-SPICED PITA CHIPS

In small bowl, combine 2 teaspoons chili powder, ½ teaspoon kosher salt, ¼ teaspoon garlic powder, and pinch cayenne pepper. In step 3, use chili mixture instead of salt.

HOW A CIRCLE BECOMES 8 TRIANGLES

To turn round pita breads into triangular chips, think of each pita as a pizza or a pie that you cut into wedges. Here's how to turn each circle into eight triangles.

1. Cut stack of pitas in half from top to bottom and then again from side to side. You should now have four same-size, triangle-shaped pieces.

2. Keep pieces together in circle and cut on diagonal through middles of triangles. You are cutting each large triangle in half to produce eight smaller, equally sized triangles.

GRAHAM CRACKERS

Makes 24 crackers | Total Time: 1 hour, plus cooling time

PREPARE INGREDIENTS

- ¾ cup (4⅛ ounces) graham flour or whole-wheat flour
- ¼ cup (1¼ ounces) all-purpose flour
- ¼ cup (1¾ ounces) sugar
- ½ teaspoon baking powder
- ¼ teaspoon baking soda
- ¼ teaspoon salt
- ⅛ teaspoon ground cinnamon
- 4 tablespoons unsalted butter, cut into ½-inch pieces and chilled
- 2 tablespoons water
- 1 tablespoon honey
- ½ teaspoon vanilla extract

GATHER COOKING EQUIPMENT

Food processor

Rubber spatula

Bench scraper or chef's knife

Plastic wrap

Parchment paper

Rolling pin

Ruler

Fork

2 rimmed baking sheets

Oven mitts

2 cooling racks

"WE ATE THEM WITH MARSHMALLOWS AND CHOCOLATE!!" - ZACHARY, 10

START COOKING!

1 Adjust oven rack to middle position and heat oven to 375 degrees.

2 Add graham flour, all-purpose flour, sugar, baking powder, baking soda, salt, and cinnamon to food processor. Lock lid into place. Turn on processor and process until well combined, about 3 seconds. Stop food processor and remove lid.

3 Sprinkle chilled butter over flour mixture and lock lid back into place. Turn on processor and process until mixture resembles coarse meal, about 15 seconds. Stop food processor and remove lid.

4 Add water, honey, and vanilla and lock lid back into place. Turn on processor and process until dough forms ball, 30 to 60 seconds. Stop processor, remove lid, and carefully remove processor blade (ask an adult for help).

5 Use rubber spatula to transfer dough to clean counter. Use bench scraper to divide dough into 2 even pieces. Wrap 1 piece of dough in plastic wrap and set aside.

6 Place remaining piece of dough in center of large piece of parchment paper. Place second large sheet of parchment on top of dough. Use rolling pin to roll and shape dough into graham crackers following photos, page 87.

7 Slide dough (still on parchment) onto baking sheet. Place baking sheet in oven. Bake until graham crackers are golden brown, 8 to 12 minutes.

8 While first batch of graham crackers is baking, repeat rolling and shaping with remaining piece of dough and 2 more sheets of parchment to make 9 more graham crackers. Slide dough onto second baking sheet.

KEEP GOING →

WHAT IS GRAHAM FLOUR?

Graham crackers are named for their inventor, Sylvester Graham, a hotel owner in the early 1800s. He created a new kind of flour, which, no surprise, he called Graham flour. Graham flour is a coarse, nutty whole-wheat flour that's made by finely grinding winter wheat. It's the traditional choice for nutty, slightly sweet Graham crackers. Don't worry if you can't find graham flour in your market; whole-wheat flour works in this recipe as well.

try it this way
CINNAMON–SUGAR GRAHAM CRACKERS

Increase cinnamon to ¼ teaspoon. Then, for topping, combine 2 tablespoons sugar and additional ½ teaspoon cinnamon in small bowl and stir to combine. In step 7, sprinkle half of cinnamon-sugar mixture on top of first baking sheet of graham crackers just before baking. In step 8, sprinkle remaining cinnamon-sugar mixture on top of second baking sheet of graham crackers just before baking.

→ **9** Use oven mitts to remove first baking sheet of crackers from oven (ask an adult for help) and place on cooling rack. Place second baking sheet in oven and bake until graham crackers are golden brown, 8 to 12 minutes. Use oven mitts to remove second baking sheet of crackers from oven and place on second cooling rack. Let crackers cool completely on baking sheets, about 30 minutes.

10 Use your hands to gently break graham crackers apart along lines. Serve. (Crackers can be stored at room temperature in airtight container for up to 2 weeks.)

HOW TO SHAPE GRAHAM CRACKERS

This dough is soft and malleable, so it is easy to patch, roll, and reroll it to get the right size and shape.

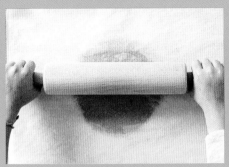

1. Use rolling pin to roll dough into 8-inch square (about ⅛ inch thick), rolling dough between sheets of parchment paper.

2. While rolling dough, if square shape is uneven, remove top piece parchment. Use bench scraper to cut off edges, then patch and press dough scraps to fill in square.

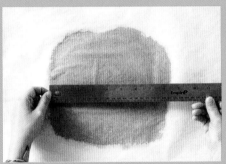

3. Place top piece of parchment back on top and continue rolling to finish reaching 8-inch square.

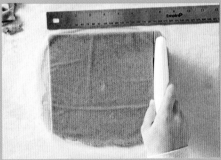

4. Remove top piece of parchment. Use bench scraper to cut off edges of dough to form tidy 7½-inch square.

5. Use bench scraper to gently cut dough into nine 2½-inch squares (do not separate squares after cutting).

6. Prick each square several times with fork.

CHEDDAR FISH CRACKERS

Makes 100 to 125 crackers | Total Time: 1 hour, plus cooling time

White cheddar works in this recipe, but we prefer the orange color of yellow cheddar. You can use sharp or extra-sharp cheddar. You can find fish cracker cutters online or at arts and crafts stores. If you can't find one, you can use any 1-inch cookie cutter you like.

PREPARE INGREDIENTS

- ¾ cup shredded extra-sharp yellow cheddar cheese (3 ounces)
- ½ cup (2½ ounces) all-purpose flour, plus extra for counter
- 1 teaspoon cornstarch
- ⅛ teaspoon salt
- 3 tablespoons unsalted butter, cut into 3 pieces and chilled
- 1 tablespoon cold water

GATHER COOKING EQUIPMENT

Rimmed baking sheet

Parchment paper

Food processor

Rolling pin

Ruler

Fish cracker cutter

Oven mitts

Cooling rack

"MY WHOLE FAMILY LOVED THEM!"

- CHARLOTTE, 8

START COOKING!

1 Line rimmed baking sheet with parchment paper. Add cheddar, flour, cornstarch, and salt to food processor and lock lid into place. Turn on processor and process until mixture is smooth, about 30 seconds. Stop processor and remove lid.

2 Add chilled butter to food processor, lock lid back into place, and process until mixture looks like wet sand, about 20 seconds. Stop processor and remove lid.

3 Add water to processor and lock lid back into place. Hold down pulse button for 1 second, then release. Repeat until dough forms large clumps, about five 1-second pulses.

4 Remove lid and carefully remove processor blade (ask an adult for help). Sprinkle clean counter lightly with extra flour. Transfer dough to lightly floured counter.

5 Gently knead dough for about 20 seconds, then roll and cut dough into fish shapes, following photos, page 90.

6 Sprinkle counter lightly with more flour. Gather dough scraps together and repeat rolling and cutting dough until only tiny scraps remain (discard scraps).

7 Place baking sheet in refrigerator and chill cut dough for 20 minutes. Meanwhile, adjust oven rack to middle position and heat oven to 350 degrees.

8 Once dough is chilled, place baking sheet in oven and bake until crackers are puffed and firm, 14 to 16 minutes.

9 Use oven mitts to remove baking sheet from oven (ask an adult for help). Place baking sheet on cooling rack. Let crackers cool completely on baking sheet, about 15 minutes. Serve. (Crackers can be stored at room temperature in airtight container for up to 1 week.)

KEEP GOING →

"COLD" FISH CRACKERS

Why is refrigerating the fish before baking them so important? It helps them keep their fishy shape! We roll out the dough straight from the food processor because the warm butter in the dough makes it soft and pliable. But when we baked the crackers immediately, they looked more like blobs than fish. Refrigerating the dough firms the butter up again. That way, when the fishies hit the oven, their fins stay fit!

try it this way
PIZZA FISH CRACKERS

In step 1, add ½ teaspoon dried oregano, ¼ teaspoon onion powder, and ¼ teaspoon garlic powder to food processor along with cheddar. In step 3, use 1 teaspoon tomato paste instead of water.

PARMESAN-ROSEMARY FISH CRACKERS

Use ⅓ cup shredded extra-sharp white cheddar and ⅓ cup grated Parmesan instead of the extra-sharp yellow cheddar. In step 1, add 1 teaspoon minced fresh rosemary to food processor along with cheeses.

CHEDDAR FISH CRACKERS

HOW TO SHAPE CHEDDAR FISH CRACKERS

1. Transfer dough to lightly floured counter. Gently knead dough together, about 20 seconds.

2. Use rolling pin to roll dough into rough 10-inch circle, about ⅛ inch thick, rotating dough a quarter turn and reflouring counter between rolls as needed.

3. Use fish cracker cutter to cut out fish as close together as you can.

4. Place fish on parchment paper–lined baking sheet (they can be close together but not touching).

don't forget to
sprinkle flour
on the counter

SEEDED CRACKERS

Makes 30 crackers | Total Time: 1½ hours, plus cooling time

PREPARE INGREDIENTS

- ½ cup (2½ ounces) all-purpose flour
- ½ cup (2¾ ounces) whole-wheat flour
- 2 tablespoons sesame seeds
- 1 tablespoon sugar
- ¾ teaspoon salt
- 4 tablespoons unsalted butter, cut into ¼-inch pieces and chilled
- ¼ cup (2 ounces) cold water
- ⅛ teaspoon plus ⅛ teaspoon kosher or flake sea salt (for sprinkling), measured separately

GATHER COOKING EQUIPMENT

2 rimmed baking sheets

Parchment paper

Large bowl

Whisk

Rubber spatula

Plastic wrap

1-teaspoon measuring spoon

1-cup dry measuring cup

Ruler

Fork

Oven mitts

2 cooling racks

"THEY WERE EASY AND FUN TO MAKE AND TASTED LIKE SWEET GRAIN." – MATTHEW, 10

START COOKING!

1 Adjust oven rack to middle position and heat oven to 350 degrees. Line 2 rimmed baking sheets with parchment paper.

2 In large bowl, whisk together all-purpose flour, whole-wheat flour, sesame seeds, sugar, and ¾ teaspoon salt.

3 Add chilled butter to flour mixture. Use your fingertips to rub butter into flour mixture until it resembles coarse meal with a few slightly larger butter lumps.

4 Add cold water and use rubber spatula to stir and press mixture until dough starts to form. Use your hands to knead mixture in bowl until dough comes together, about 30 seconds.

5 Cover with plastic wrap, place bowl in refrigerator, and chill until no longer sticky, about 20 minutes.

6 Roll and shape 15 crackers following photos, page 94. Sprinkle crackers evenly with ⅛ teaspoon kosher salt.

7 Place baking sheet in oven. Bake until crackers are browned around edges, 22 to 24 minutes. While your first baking sheet of crackers is baking, repeat rolling and shaping the remaining dough and sprinkle with remaining ⅛ teaspoon kosher salt to make 15 more crackers on second baking sheet.

8 Use oven mitts to remove first baking sheet of crackers from oven (ask an adult for help) and place on cooling rack. Place second baking sheet in oven and bake until crackers are browned around edges, 22 to 24 minutes. Use oven mitts to remove second baking sheet of crackers from oven and place on second cooling rack.

9 Let crackers cool completely on baking sheets, about 15 minutes. Serve. Crackers can be stored at room temperature in airtight container for up to 2 days.)

KEEP GOING →

try it this way

EVERYTHING CRACKERS

Instead of sesame seeds, add 2 tablespoons Everything Bagel Seasoning (see recipe, page 74) to bowl along with flours, sugar, and salt in step 2. Omit kosher salt.

they are extra delicious with cheese

93

HOW TO SHAPE CRACKERS

1. Working with 1 heaping teaspoon dough at a time, use your hands to roll dough into 15 balls and space them evenly on parchment–lined baking sheet. Cover baking sheet loosely with plastic wrap.

2. Use bottom of 1-cup dry measuring cup to press each dough ball very flat and thin. The crackers should be 2 to 2½ inches in diameter. Discard plastic wrap.

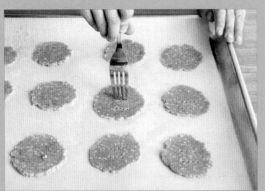

3. Use fork to prick each cracker twice.

PRESSING (CRACKER) QUESTIONS

Most cracker recipes call for rolling dough out into a very flat, very thin, very even layer . . . and then cutting it into uniform shapes. Talk about a lot of work! Instead, we measure out individual crackers and use a dry measuring cup to press them into thin, even little rounds. Press away!

use your hands
to roll the
dough into balls

CARAMEL POPCORN

Makes 7½ cups | Total Time: 1 hour and 30 minutes, plus cooling time

Use plain popcorn in this recipe, not popcorn with butter flavoring. Make sure to use dark corn syrup here. Light corn syrup won't give you that deep caramel-y color.

PREPARE INGREDIENTS

Vegetable oil spray

7 cups popped plain popcorn

5 tablespoons unsalted butter

¾ cup packed light brown sugar

¼ cup dark corn syrup

¼ teaspoon salt

¾ teaspoon vanilla extract

¼ teaspoon baking soda

½ cup salted peanuts (optional)

GATHER COOKING EQUIPMENT

13-by-9-inch metal baking pan

Large saucepan

Rubber spatula

Oven mitts

Cooling rack

" WHEN I WAS STIRRING THE CARAMEL I LIKED WATCHING AS IT GOT THICKER." – COLETTE, 10

START COOKING!

1 Adjust oven rack to middle position and heat oven to 250 degrees. Spray inside bottom and sides of 13-by-9-inch metal baking pan with vegetable oil spray. Place popcorn in baking pan.

2 In large saucepan, melt butter over medium-high heat. Add brown sugar, corn syrup, and salt to saucepan. Bring mixture to boil. Reduce heat to medium-low and simmer, stirring occasionally with rubber spatula, until mixture thickens slightly, about 3 minutes. Turn off heat and slide saucepan to cool burner.

3 Carefully add vanilla and baking soda (mixture will bubble and foam). Add peanuts (if using) and stir to combine.

4 Ask an adult to use rubber spatula to carefully scrape caramel mixture onto popcorn in baking pan (saucepan will be heavy and caramel will be hot). Use rubber spatula to gently stir until popcorn is evenly coated. Spread popcorn into even layer.

5 Place baking pan in oven and bake for 20 minutes. Use oven mitts to remove baking pan from oven (ask an adult for help). Place baking pan on cooling rack. Use rubber spatula to carefully stir popcorn, scraping up caramel from bottom of pan (pan will be hot). Spread popcorn back into even layer.

6 Return baking pan to oven and bake until popcorn is deep golden brown, about 40 minutes, repeating stirring halfway through baking.

7 Use oven mitts to remove baking pan from oven (ask an adult for help). Place baking pan on cooling rack and carefully stir popcorn one last time (pan will be hot). Let caramel popcorn cool completely in pan, about 30 minutes. Break popcorn apart with your hands and serve. (Caramel popcorn can be stored at room temperature in airtight container for up to 5 days.)

POPCORN WITH WINGS... OR A CAP!

Did you know that popcorn comes in different shapes? There are two main kinds: butterfly (also called snowflake) and mushroom. Most of the popcorn you get at the movies or buy as kernels in the supermarket is the butterfly shape, which pops up light and fluffy with lots of "wings" sticking out. Caramel popcorn, however, is often made with mushroom popcorn, which has a rounder shape (like a mushroom with a cap) and a more sturdy texture. Both popcorn shapes work for this recipe, but if you find mushroom popcorn in a specialty store or online, give it a try in caramel popcorn!

butterfly

mushroom

NUT AND SEED GRANOLA

Makes about 5 cups | Total Time: 1 hour, plus cooling time

PREPARE INGREDIENTS

Vegetable oil spray

¼ cup extra-virgin olive oil

¼ cup maple syrup

3 tablespoons packed light brown sugar

2 teaspoons vanilla extract

¾ teaspoon flake sea salt

2½ cups (7½ ounces) old-fashioned rolled oats

¾ cup raw pepitas

¾ cup (1½ ounces) unsweetened flaked coconut

½ cup pecans, chopped fine

GATHER COOKING EQUIPMENT

13-by-9-inch metal baking pan

Large bowl

Rubber spatula

Oven mitts

Cooling rack

> " IT HAS EVERYTHING I LIKE: PUMPKIN SEEDS AND GRANOLA!"
> – ADIA, 11

START COOKING!

1 Adjust oven rack to middle position and heat oven to 325 degrees. Spray inside bottom and sides of 13-by-9-inch metal baking pan with vegetable oil spray.

2 In large bowl, combine oil, maple syrup, brown sugar, vanilla, and salt. Use rubber spatula to stir until well combined. Add oats, pepitas, coconut, and pecans and stir until evenly coated with oil mixture.

3 Transfer oat mixture to greased baking pan and use rubber spatula to spread mixture into even layer. Use rubber spatula to press down firmly on oat mixture until mixture is very flat (see photo, right).

4 Place baking pan in oven. Bake until lightly browned, 25 to 30 minutes.

5 Use oven mitts to remove baking pan from oven (ask an adult for help). Place baking pan on cooling rack and let granola cool completely in pan, about 45 minutes.

6 Use your hands to break cooled granola into bite-size pieces. Serve. (Granola can be stored at room temperature in airtight container for up to 2 weeks.)

HOW TO PACK YOUR GRANOLA

The key to getting big, crunchy bites is to pack the oat mixture into the pan before you bake it.

Use rubber spatula to spread oat mixture into even layer. Use rubber spatula to press down firmly on oat mixture until mixture is very flat.

try it this way
NUT-FREE GRANOLA

Use ½ cup raw sunflower seeds instead of pecans.

SWEET AND SALTY PEPITAS

Makes 1 cup | Total Time: 10 minutes, plus cooling time

Make sure to use raw pepitas in this recipe.

PREPARE INGREDIENTS

- 1 cup raw pepitas
- 2 teaspoons sugar
- 1 teaspoon extra-virgin olive oil
- 1 teaspoon kosher salt

GATHER COOKING EQUIPMENT

12-inch skillet

Rubber spatula

Serving bowl

" THE PERFECT SNACK."

-SARAH, 9

START COOKING!

1 Add pepitas to 12-inch skillet and place over medium-low heat. Cook, stirring constantly with rubber spatula, until puffed and golden, 6 to 8 minutes.

2 Turn off heat and slide skillet to cool burner. Add sugar, oil, and salt and stir to combine.

3 Let pepitas cool in skillet for 15 minutes. Transfer pepitas to serving bowl. Serve. (Pepitas can be stored at room temperature in airtight container for up to 1 week.)

WHAT MAKES A PEPITA POP?

Toasting pepitas, which are squash seeds, gives them a nice nutty flavor. Toasting also causes them to puff up and become crispy. And occasionally a toasted pepita will POP. Why? Much like dried corn kernels used for popcorn, fresh pepitas contain moisture. When heated, the moisture turns to steam, and building pressure will cause the steam to escape from the seed in the form of a pop. Take care when toasting pepitas: It's a safe assumption that if a pepita pops, it's hot!

try it this way
GINGER-SOY PEPITAS

Place oil in small bowl. Reduce sugar to 1 teaspoon and leave out salt. Add sugar, 1 tablespoon soy sauce, and ¼ teaspoon ground ginger to bowl with oil and stir until sugar is dissolved. In step 2, pour mixture over toasted pepitas in skillet and stir to combine.

MAPLE-CHILI PEPITAS

Place oil in small bowl. Reduce salt to ½ teaspoon and leave out sugar. Add salt, 1 tablespoon maple syrup, 1 teaspoon chili powder, and ¼ teaspoon ground cumin to bowl with oil and stir until salt is dissolved. In step 2, pour mixture over toasted pepitas in skillet and stir to combine.

CRANBERRY–ALMOND ENERGY BARS

Makes 12 bars | Total Time: 20 minutes, plus 1 hour chilling time

PREPARE INGREDIENTS

- 2 cups whole almonds
- ¼ teaspoon salt
- 1½ cups dried cranberries
- 1½ cups chopped pitted dates
- 2 tablespoons water
- ¼ teaspoon vanilla extract

GATHER COOKING EQUIPMENT

8-inch square metal baking pan

Plastic wrap

Food processor

Rubber spatula

Cutting board

Chef's knife

"IT WAS REALLY GOOD!
I HOPE I GET HEALTHY FROM IT."
– PARKER, 9

START COOKING!

1 Line 8-inch square metal baking pan with plastic wrap, letting excess hang over sides of pan.

2 Add almonds and salt to food processor and lock lid into place. Turn on processor and process until almonds are finely ground, 20 to 30 seconds. Stop processor and remove lid.

3 Add cranberries, dates, water, and vanilla to processor and lock lid back into place. Hold down pulse button for 1 second, then release. Repeat until fruit is finely chopped and mixture starts to clump together, about fifteen 1-second pulses. Stop processor, remove lid, and carefully remove processor blade (ask an adult for help).

4 Use rubber spatula to transfer mixture to plastic-lined baking pan and spread into even layer. Fold excess plastic over top and use your hands to press mixture firmly to flatten (see photo, right).

5 Place baking pan in refrigerator and chill until firm, about 1 hour.

6 Transfer chilled mixture to cutting board and discard plastic. Slice in half, then cut each half crosswise into 6 pieces (you should have 12 bars). Serve. (Bars can be refrigerated in airtight container for up to 1 week.)

HOW TO SHAPE ENERGY BARS

Use rubber spatula to transfer mixture to plastic-lined baking pan and spread into even layer. Fold excess plastic over top and, using your hands, press mixture firmly to flatten.

RAW BARS?!

There are all kinds of raw fruit and nut bars packaged in bright colors and sold at the supermarket. They are simple and delicious, packed with protein from the nuts and sweetness from the dried fruit. The best part? They require no cooking to make. All you need is a food processor to finely chop the ingredients. Then you press the mixture into a pan, chill it, and slice it into bars. Done!

STRAWBERRY POP TARTS

Makes 8 pop tarts | Total Time: 2½ hours, plus cooling time

PREPARE INGREDIENTS

- ½ cup sour cream, chilled
- 1 large egg
- 2½ cups (12½ ounces) all-purpose flour, plus extra for counter
- 1 tablespoon sugar
- 1 teaspoon salt
- 12 tablespoons unsalted butter, cut into ½-inch pieces and chilled
- ¾ cup strawberry jam
- 1 tablespoon cornstarch
- 1 tablespoon cold water

GATHER COOKING EQUIPMENT

2 small bowls (1 microwave-safe)

Whisk

Food processor

Bench scraper or chef's knife

Ruler

Plastic wrap

Oven mitts

Rimmed baking sheet

Parchment paper

Rolling pin

Fork

1-tablespoon measuring spoon

Cooling rack

START COOKING!

1 In small bowl, whisk together sour cream and egg. Set aside. In food processor, combine flour, sugar, and salt. Lock lid into place. Turn on processor and process for 3 seconds. Stop processor.

2 Remove lid and sprinkle chilled butter over flour mixture. Lock lid back into place. Hold down pulse button for 1 second, then release. Repeat until only pea-size pieces of butter remain, about ten 1-second pulses.

3 Remove lid and add sour cream mixture. Lock lid back into place and pulse until just combined, about ten 1-second pulses.

4 Turn on processor and process until dough forms ball, 10 to 15 seconds. Stop processor, remove lid, and carefully remove processor blade (ask an adult for help).

5 Sprinkle counter lightly with extra flour. Transfer dough to floured counter and press together into ball. Use bench scraper to divide dough in half.

6 Use your hands to form each piece of dough into 3-by-5-inch rectangle. Wrap each rectangle tightly in plastic wrap. Place in refrigerator and chill for 1 hour.

7 While dough chills, in small microwave-safe bowl, combine jam, cornstarch, and water. Whisk until combined and no cornstarch is visible. Heat in microwave until mixture begins to form small bubbles, about 2 minutes. Use oven mitts to remove bowl from microwave (ask an adult for help). Whisk mixture until well combined. Set aside to cool.

8 Remove chilled dough from refrigerator and let sit on counter to soften slightly before rolling, about 10 minutes. Line rimmed baking sheet with parchment paper.

KEEP GOING →

HOW TO FROST POP TARTS

If you want frosted treats, you can make a quick icing for your pop tarts.

To make icing
In small bowl, whisk 1¼ cups (5 ounces) confectioners' sugar, 2 tablespoons milk, and 1 tablespoon softened cream cheese until smooth.

To frost
Spread 1 teaspoon icing onto each cooled pop tart. You can also sprinkle your frosted pop tarts with Sprinkles (page 148)! (Frosted pop tarts can be reheated in toaster oven on lowest setting for 1 to 2 minutes. Do not reheat frosted pop tarts in upright toaster, as frosting may melt.)

→ **9** Sprinkle counter lightly with extra flour. Roll, cut, fill, and shape each rectangle of dough to make 8 pop tarts, following photos, right.

10 Place baking sheet with shaped pop tarts in refrigerator and chill for 15 minutes. Meanwhile, adjust oven rack to middle position and heat oven to 350 degrees.

11 Place baking sheet in oven and bake until pop tart edges are just beginning to brown, 20 to 24 minutes.

12 Use oven mitts to remove baking sheet from oven (ask an adult for help). Place baking sheet on cooling rack and let pop tarts cool on baking sheet for at least 30 minutes. Serve. (Pop tarts can be stored at room temperature in airtight container for up to 2 days. Pop tarts can be reheated in toaster on lowest setting for 1 to 2 minutes.)

THE ORIGINAL TART

Did you know that the classic brand of these frosted hand pies—Pop Tarts—are more than 50 years old?! The original Pop Tarts' claim to fame was that they contained fruit filling but did not have to be refrigerated. When they first hit supermarket shelves, there were no frosted varieties. It took a few years for the company to develop a frosting that could withstand the heat of the toaster!

HOW TO SHAPE POP TARTS

1. Use rolling pin to roll 1 piece of dough into 12½-by-9½-inch rectangle on floured counter.

2. Use bench scraper to cut off edges of dough to form tidy 12-by-9-inch rectangle. Use bench scraper to cut dough into eight 3-by-4½-inch rectangles.

3. Place 8 rectangles onto parchment-lined baking sheet. (These will be the bottoms of your pop tarts.) Place baking sheet in refrigerator to chill while rolling second piece of dough.

4. Repeat rolling and cutting with second piece of dough. Use fork to poke 2 rows of holes in each rectangle. (These will be the tops of your pop tarts.)

5. Remove baking sheet with bottoms from refrigerator. Use measuring spoon to place 1 level tablespoon of cooled jam mixture in center of each bottom rectangle on baking sheet. Dip your finger in water and lightly moisten edges of each rectangle.

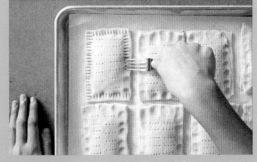

6. Place 1 top rectangle onto each bottom rectangle, making sure all edges are lined up. Use your fingers to firmly press top and bottom edges of rectangles together to seal. Use fork to press sealed edges together to crimp dough.

TRIPLE-BERRY FRUIT LEATHER

Makes 12 fruit strips | Total Time: 5 to 6 hours, plus cooling time

You can substitute frozen berries for the fresh berries if you want.

PREPARE INGREDIENTS

Vegetable oil spray

4 cups mixed berries (blueberries, raspberries, and strawberries—strawberries hulled and chopped, see page 29)

2 large Granny Smith apples (8 ounces each), peeled, cored, and chopped

¼ cup sugar

GATHER COOKING EQUIPMENT

Pencil

Ruler

Parchment paper

Rimless baking sheet

Blender

Rubber spatula

Fine-mesh strainer

Large saucepan

Ladle

Whisk

4-cup liquid measuring cup

Icing spatula

Oven mitts

Cooling rack

Scissors

"IT SMELLED SO GOOD WHILE COOKING. IT'S AMAZING HOW IT CHANGED COLORS."
— SELAH, 10

START COOKING!

1 Adjust oven rack to middle position and heat oven to 200 degrees. Use pencil and ruler to draw 14-by-11-inch rectangle on large sheet of parchment paper. Flip parchment and place on rimless baking sheet. Spray parchment evenly with vegetable oil spray.

2 Place berries in blender jar followed by apples. Place lid on top of blender and hold lid firmly in place with folded dish towel (see page 38). Hold down pulse button for 1 second, then release. Repeat until fruit is finely chopped, about ten 1-second pulses, scraping down sides of blender jar with rubber spatula a few times.

3 Add sugar and replace lid. Process until very smooth, about 3 minutes, stopping to scrape down sides of blender jar with rubber spatula halfway through processing.

4 Place fine-mesh strainer over large saucepan. Pour berry mixture through strainer into saucepan. Use back of ladle to stir and press on mixture to get out as much liquid as possible; discard solids in strainer.

5 Bring mixture to boil over medium-high heat. Reduce heat to medium-low and gently simmer, whisking often and lowering heat if mixture begins to splatter, until mixture is thickened, about 30 minutes.

6 Ask an adult to help pour mixture into 4-cup liquid measuring cup. Mixture should measure 2 cups. If it is more than 2 cups, return mixture to saucepan and continue to cook over medium-low heat until mixture measures 2 cups.

7 Carefully pour berry mixture onto center of parchment-lined baking sheet (ask an adult for help) and spread into smooth, even layer following photos, right.

KEEP GOING →

HOW TO SHAPE FRUIT LEATHER

1. Pour berry mixture onto center of parchment-lined baking sheet (ask an adult for help).

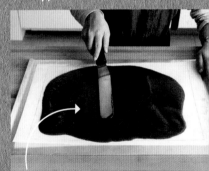

2. Use icing spatula to spread mixture into even layer to edges of 14-by-11-inch rectangle. Gently jiggle and tap baking sheet on counter to create smooth, even layer.

MORE!
TRIPLE-BERRY FRUIT LEATHER

→ **8** Place baking sheet in oven and bake until mixture is set, 4 to 5 hours. To check for doneness, use oven mitts to remove baking sheet from oven and place on cooling rack (ask an adult for help). Gently touch center of fruit leather—it should feel dry but slightly tacky to touch, and fruit leather should peel away from parchment cleanly. (If it's still too wet, use oven mitts to transfer baking sheet back to oven and continue baking.)

9 Let fruit leather cool completely, about 30 minutes. Use scissors to cut fruit leather (along with parchment backing) crosswise into twelve 1-inch-wide strips (trimming away any dry edges as needed). Roll up fruit leather strips. Serve. (Fruit leather can be stored at room temperature in airtight container for up to 2 weeks.)

FIRST FRUIT LEATHER

Have you ever eaten Fruit Roll-Ups? These chewy, fruity treats are produced by General Mills and have been in supermarkets since 1983. That's a long time. But rolled fruit snacks have actually been around far longer. More than a hundred years ago in New York City, a Syrian immigrant imported apricot paste and turned it into a fruit leather called amardeen. It came in large sheets, so when a customer wanted to buy some, they simply cut off a long piece and handed it to them.

try it this way
STRAWBERRY FRUIT LEATHER

Use 4 cups strawberries, hulled and chopped, instead of mixed berries.

RASPBERRY FRUIT LEATHER

Use 4 cups raspberries instead of mixed berries.

kitchen shears
make the job
quick and easy

CHEWY LEMONADE FRUIT SNACKS

Makes 72 fruit snacks | Total Time: 1 hour, plus chilling time

Our favorite frozen juice concentrate for these fruit snacks is lemonade, but pink lemonade or limeade concentrates work well, too. Don't use orange or grapefruit juice concentrates—they are too thick. We love lemon slice molds, but any 1-inch-wide by ½-inch-deep silicone molds will work.

PREPARE INGREDIENTS

- ½ cup thawed lemonade concentrate
- 1 tablespoon lemon juice, squeezed from ½ lemon
- 2 teaspoons sugar
- 2 tablespoons unflavored gelatin

GATHER COOKING EQUIPMENT

Medium microwave-safe bowl

Rubber spatula

Oven mitts

2 silicone lemon slice molds

Rimmed baking sheet or flat platter

Eyedropper

Airtight container

“ **A REALLY COOL TEXTURE AND TASTES GREAT!"**

- TREVOR, 12

START COOKING!

1 In medium microwave-safe bowl, combine thawed lemonade concentrate, lemon juice, and sugar. Sprinkle gelatin over surface of liquid. Use rubber spatula to stir until no large lumps remain. Let mixture sit for 5 minutes.

2 Heat lemonade mixture in microwave for 1 minute. Stir mixture with rubber spatula. Heat in microwave until mixture bubbles and foams, about 1 more minute.

3 Use oven mitts to remove bowl from microwave (ask an adult for help—mixture will be VERY hot). Stir mixture until fully combined and smooth.

4 Place 2 silicone lemon slice molds on rimmed baking sheet. Use eyedropper to fill molds following photos, right.

5 Place baking sheet with filled molds in refrigerator. Chill until lemonade mixture is firm, about 30 minutes.

6 Remove baking sheet with molds from refrigerator. Push each shape inside out to remove fruit snacks, and transfer to airtight container.

7 Heat remaining lemonade mixture in microwave until warmed through and liquid again, about 30 seconds. Repeat steps 4 through 6 using clean eyedropper and molds and remaining warm lemonade mixture. Serve. (Fruit snacks can be refrigerated in airtight container for up to 1 week.)

HOW TO FILL MOLDS

1. Dip tip of eyedropper into warm lemonade mixture. Squeeze and let go of bulb to fill eyedropper.

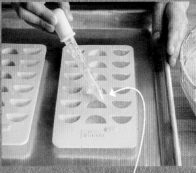

2. Hold filled eyedropper over shape in mold and gently squeeze bulb to fill shape to top with lemonade mixture. Repeat until all shapes are filled in both molds.

PUTTING THE "CHEW" IN CHEWY FRUIT SNACKS

Fruit snacks have a unique texture. They're bouncy—you can gently squeeze them and they'll pop back into shape—but not sticky. They're chewy but also soft enough that you can easily bite into them. How do they get this special texture? From a kind of protein called gelatin. Here's how it works: The powdered gelatin dissolved when you stirred it into the lemonade concentrate and heated the mixture in the microwave. Then, as the gelatin-lemonade mixture cooled in the refrigerator, the gelatin proteins formed a tangled net that trapped tiny drops of the lemonade inside. When the mixture cooled down enough, it turned from a liquid to a solid.

PARMESAN TWISTS

Makes 14 twists | Total Time: 1 hour

Be sure to let the frozen puff pastry thaw completely before using it; otherwise, it can crack and fall apart. To thaw frozen puff pastry, let it sit either in the refrigerator for 24 hours or on the counter for 30 minutes to 1 hour.

PREPARE INGREDIENTS

Vegetable oil spray

All-purpose flour (for sprinkling on counter)

1 (9½-by-9-inch) sheet puff pastry, thawed

2 tablespoons butter, melted and cooled (see page 14)

¼ teaspoon salt

½ cup plus ¼ cup grated Parmesan cheese, measured separately

GATHER COOKING EQUIPMENT

Rimmed baking sheet

Parchment paper

Rolling pin

Ruler

Pastry brush

Bench scraper or chef's knife

Oven mitts

Cooling rack

Spatula

❝ DELICIOUS AND A LOVELY BALANCE BETWEEN PASTRY, SALT, AND CHEESE." – SYLVIA, 11

START COOKING!

1 Adjust oven rack to upper-middle position and heat oven to 400 degrees. Line rimmed baking sheet with parchment paper. Spray parchment lightly with vegetable oil spray.

2 Sprinkle clean counter lightly with flour. Place puff pastry on counter. Use rolling pin to roll into 10½-inch square.

3 Use pastry brush to paint puff pastry evenly with melted butter. Sprinkle salt and ½ cup Parmesan evenly over top, making sure to reach edges of pastry. Use your hands to press firmly on cheese so it sticks to puff pastry.

4 Use bench scraper to cut pastry into 14 strips, about ¾ inch wide, and shape into twists following photos, right. Place twists on greased parchment-lined baking sheet.

5 Sprinkle twists evenly with remaining ¼ cup Parmesan. Place baking sheet in oven. Bake until twists are puffed and deep golden, 16 to 20 minutes.

6 Use oven mitts to remove baking sheet from oven (ask an adult for help). Place baking sheet on cooling rack and let twists cool on baking sheet for 10 minutes.

7 Use spatula to loosen twists from baking sheet. Serve warm or at room temperature. (Twists can be stored at room temperature in airtight container for up to 3 days.)

PUFF THE MAGIC PASTRY

Puff pastry is an almost magical ingredient that starts out flat and puffs up into a flaky crust in the oven. It's made from layers and layers of dough and butter stacked on top of each other. As the butter heats up in the oven, it lets off steam, which pushes the dough layers apart to make an ultraflaky texture. You can make your own puff pastry, but it's a **LOT** of work. Instead, we like to buy frozen premade puff pastry at the grocery store.

HOW TO TWIST

1. Use ruler and bench scraper to mark top and bottom of puff pastry every ¾ inch.

2. Use bench scraper to cut pastry from mark to mark into strips.

3. Hold middle of 1 strip with fingertips and twist in opposite directions to make spiral. Continue twisting a few times until you reach ends of strip.

chapter 3

SWEETS

VANILLA NO-CHURN ICE CREAM

Makes 1 quart | Total Time: 20 minutes, plus 6 hours freezing time

This ice cream freezes more quickly in a loaf pan than in a taller, narrower container. If you don't have a loaf pan, use an 8-inch square metal baking pan.

PREPARE INGREDIENTS

- 2 cups heavy cream, chilled
- 1 cup sweetened condensed milk
- ¼ cup whole milk
- ¼ cup light corn syrup
- 2 tablespoons sugar
- 1 tablespoon vanilla extract
- ¼ teaspoon salt

GATHER COOKING EQUIPMENT

Blender

Dish towel

Rubber spatula

8½-by-4½-inch metal loaf pan

Plastic wrap

" SOOOO CREAMY!"
-NATHAN, 8

START COOKING!

1 Add cream to blender jar. Place lid on top of blender and hold lid firmly in place with folded dish towel (see page 38). Turn on blender and process until soft peaks form, 20 to 30 seconds. Stop blender and remove lid.

2 Use rubber spatula to scrape down sides of blender jar. Replace lid and continue to process until stiff peaks form, about 10 seconds (see photo, right). Stop blender and remove lid.

3 Add condensed milk, whole milk, corn syrup, sugar, vanilla, and salt to blender. Use rubber spatula to stir into whipped cream. Replace lid and process until well combined, about 20 seconds. Stop blender and remove lid.

4 Pour cream mixture into 8½-by-4½-inch metal loaf pan. Cover with plastic wrap, gently pressing plastic onto surface of mixture. Place in freezer and freeze until firm, at least 6 hours. Serve. (Ice cream can be frozen in covered loaf pan for up to 1 week.)

KEEP GOING →

HERE'S THE SCOOP

An ice cream maker works by churning—slowly stirring—a mixture (usually milk, cream, sugar, and egg yolks) as it freezes. This incorporates air into the mixture, so you wind up with scoopable ice cream instead of a solid ice cube. In this recipe, whipping the cream in the blender traps lots of air inside of it. The air trapped inside the fluffy whipped cream takes the place of the air normally incorporated by an ice cream maker. Ice cream for all!

load up the ice cream with your favorite sauce and toppings!

try it this way

This ice cream recipe is endlessly adaptable. Try one of these fun flavors!

MINT COOKIE NO-CHURN ICE CREAM

Leave out vanilla extract. In step 3, add ¾ teaspoon peppermint extract and ⅛ teaspoon green food coloring to blender with sweetened condensed milk. In step 4, gently stir 4 crushed Oreo cookies into cream mixture in loaf pan before covering and freezing.

MILK CHOCOLATE NO-CHURN ICE CREAM

Reduce vanilla to 1 teaspoon. Place 1 cup milk chocolate chips in small microwave-safe bowl. Heat in microwave on 50 percent power for 1 minute. Use spoon to stir chocolate. Return bowl to microwave and heat at 50 percent power until chocolate is melted, about 1 minute. Use oven mitts to remove bowl from microwave and stir until chocolate is completely melted and smooth. Let chocolate cool slightly, about 5 minutes. In step 3, add melted chocolate to blender along with sweetened condensed milk.

PEANUT BUTTER CUP NO-CHURN ICE CREAM

Leave out vanilla extract. In step 3, add ½ cup creamy peanut butter to blender with sweetened condensed milk. In step 4, gently stir ½ cup chopped peanut butter cups into cream mixture in loaf pan before covering and freezing.

STRAWBERRY BUTTERMILK NO-CHURN ICE CREAM

Leave out vanilla extract. Use ½ cup buttermilk instead of the whole milk. In step 3, add 1 teaspoon lemon juice to blender with sweetened condensed milk. In step 4, spoon ⅓ cup strawberry jam on top of cream mixture in loaf pan and use fork to swirl into cream mixture before covering and freezing.

for even more mint flavor, swap oreos for thin mints!

RASPBERRY SORBET

Makes 1 quart | Total Time: 45 minutes, plus 14 to 36 hours freezing time

You can use fresh or frozen raspberries in this recipe. If using frozen raspberries, thaw them before using. For planning purposes, note that there are two rounds of freezing involved in making this sorbet. The first is at least 8 hours, and the second is at least 6 hours.

PREPARE INGREDIENTS

⅔ cup water

¼ cup lemon juice, squeezed from 2 lemons (see page 16)

4 cups (20 ounces) raspberries

1⅓ cups sugar

⅛ teaspoon salt

GATHER COOKING EQUIPMENT

4-cup liquid measuring cup

Food processor

Fine-mesh strainer

Large bowl

Ladle

2 ice cube trays

Butter knife

Rubber spatula

Quart-size storage container

"IT WAS FULL OF BRIGHT RASPBERRY FLAVOR."
-REX, 12

START COOKING!

1 Combine water and lemon juice in 4-cup liquid measuring cup and set aside.

2 Add raspberries, sugar, and salt to food processor. Lock lid into place. Hold down pulse button for 1 second, then release. Repeat until raspberries are broken down, about five 1-second pulses.

3 Turn on processor. With processor running, pour water mixture through feed tube (see photo, page 49). Continue to process until sugar has dissolved and mixture is smooth, about 1 minute. Stop processor. Remove lid and carefully remove processor blade (ask an adult for help).

4 Set fine-mesh strainer over large bowl. Pour raspberry mixture into fine-mesh strainer. Use ladle to stir and press mixture to push liquid through strainer into bowl. Discard solids in strainer.

5 Transfer raspberry mixture to now-empty liquid measuring cup. Pour raspberry mixture into 2 ice cube trays. Place in freezer and freeze until solid, at least 8 hours or overnight.

6 Remove ice cube trays from freezer and let sit on counter until softened slightly, 15 to 20 minutes.

KEEP GOING →

WHY A FOOD PROCESSOR?

Sorbets are traditionally made in an ice cream maker, which churns (slowly stirs) the mixture while it freezes. The mixing incorporates air into the sorbet and makes it scoopable. In this recipe, the food processor takes the place of the ice cream maker, quickly incorporating air into the mixture. But food processors don't get cold. That's why you need to pop your finished sorbet back in the freezer for a few hours before you eat it.

SORBET SCIENCE

Sorbet ("sore-BAY") is a frozen dessert usually made from fruit and sugar. The best sorbet has a soft, silky texture that melts in your mouth. The secret to sorbet's texture is . . . sugar! Sugar not only makes sorbet sweet but also makes it smooth and scoopable instead of hard and icy. How? Sugar dissolves in the liquid released from the chopped or processed fruit (which is mostly water). As the fruit-sugar mixture freezes, the dissolved sugar gets in the way of ice crystals forming in the freezing water. This also makes any ice crystals that do form very tiny and helps give your sorbet a smooth texture. In addition, the dissolved sugar lowers the freezing point of the water to below 32 degrees, which makes it more difficult for those ice crystals to form. And fewer ice crystals means more-scoopable sorbet.

try it this way
BLACKBERRY SORBET

Use 4 cups blackberries instead of raspberries. Increase lemon juice to 6 tablespoons (squeezed from 2 lemons).

RASPBERRY SORBET

→ **7** Use butter knife to loosen cubes from ice cube trays and transfer cubes to clean processor (see photo 1, below). Lock lid into place. Hold down pulse button for 1 second, then release. Repeat until cubes begin to break down, about 10 pulses.

8 Turn on processor and process until cubes are mostly broken down, about 30 seconds. Stop processor. Remove lid and use rubber spatula to scrape down sides of processor bowl and break up any cubes that are stuck together. Lock lid back into place and process until smooth, about 1 minute. Stop processor.

9 Remove lid and carefully remove processor blade (ask an adult for help). Use rubber spatula to scrape sorbet into quart-size storage container (see photo 2, below). Place in freezer and freeze until firm, about 6 hours or overnight. Serve. (Sorbet can be frozen in airtight container for up to 1 week.)

EASY FREEZY!

1. Use butter knife to loosen cubes from ice cube trays and transfer cubes to clean food processor.

2. After processing mixture in step 8, remove lid and carefully remove processor blade (ask an adult for help). Use rubber spatula to scrape sorbet into storage container.

a butter knife makes it easy to remove the cubes

CHOCOLATE CHIP COOKIE ICE CREAM SANDWICHES

Makes 6 sandwiches | Total Time: 1½ hours, plus 8 hours freezing time

Make sure to soften your ice cream in the refrigerator before you scoop it. The ice cream should be slightly softened but not soupy.

PREPARE INGREDIENTS

Vegetable oil spray

⅔ cup (3⅓ ounces) all-purpose flour

¼ teaspoon salt

⅛ teaspoon baking soda

½ cup packed (3½ ounces) brown sugar

3 tablespoons unsalted butter, melted (see page 14)

2 tablespoons water

1 large egg yolk (see page 15)

1½ teaspoons vanilla extract

¼ cup (1½ ounces) mini semisweet chocolate chips

1 quart ice cream (see page 118, or store-bought), softened

> **THE COOKIES WERE GREAT BECAUSE THEY STAYED SOFT WHEN FROZEN."**
> **-GARRICK, 13**

GATHER COOKING EQUIPMENT

Rimmed baking sheet

Parchment paper

2 bowls (1 large, 1 medium)

Whisk

Rubber spatula

1-tablespoon measuring spoon

Oven mitts

Cooling rack

Ice cream scoop
  (#16 size works well)

Large plate

START COOKING!

1 Adjust oven rack to middle position and heat oven to 325 degrees. Line rimmed baking sheet with parchment paper. Spray lightly with vegetable oil spray.

2 In medium bowl, whisk together flour, salt, and baking soda. In large bowl, whisk brown sugar, melted butter, water, egg yolk, and vanilla until smooth, about 30 seconds.

3 Add flour mixture to brown sugar mixture and use rubber spatula to stir until combined and no dry flour is visible. Stir in chocolate chips. (Dough will be very soft.)

4 Use 1-tablespoon measuring spoon to scoop 12 mounds of dough onto greased parchment-lined baking sheet (about 1 level tablespoon of dough per mound).

5 Place baking sheet in oven and bake until cookies are puffed and golden brown, 12 to 14 minutes.

6 Use oven mitts to remove baking sheet from oven (ask an adult for help). Place baking sheet on cooling rack and let cookies cool completely on baking sheet, about 30 minutes. (This is a good time to soften your ice cream in the refrigerator, 15 to 20 minutes.)

7 Fill cookies with ice cream following photos, right.

8 Freeze sandwiches until firm, at least 8 hours. Serve. (Ice cream sandwiches can be individually wrapped in plastic wrap, transferred to a zipper-lock bag, and frozen for up to 2 months.)

KEEP GOING →

HOW TO FILL ICE CREAM SANDWICHES

1. Flip 3 cooled cookies upside down on baking sheet. Use ice cream scoop to place 1 scoop of ice cream in center of each upside-down cookie (scoop of ice cream should be about 2 inches tall and 2 inches wide).

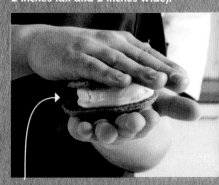

2. Working quickly, place 3 cookies, right side up, on top of ice cream to make sandwiches. Gently press cookies and twist to push ice cream to edges of cookies. Place ice cream sandwiches on large plate and place in freezer. Repeat scooping ice cream to make 3 more sandwiches with remaining cookies, then place on plate in freezer (you'll have 6 sandwiches total).

THE PERFECT (FROZEN) COOKIE

The best ice cream sandwiches aren't made with just ANY cookie. Ice cream sandwich cookies can turn rock-hard in the freezer . . . or lose all their flavor! That's why we add water to our cookie dough: It helps the cookies stay soft in the freezer. Plus, we add brown sugar, vanilla, and salt to give them extra flavor even when they're cold (which makes it harder to taste things!). Lastly, the mini chocolate chips guarantee that every bite has a burst of chocolaty flavor.

HOW TO DECORATE ICE CREAM SANDWICHES

These ice cream sandwiches are great served plain, but you can also take them to the next level by decorating the edges! Place 1 cup mini chocolate chips, chopped nuts, or sprinkles (see page 148) in shallow dish. At end of step 7, working quickly with 1 sandwich at a time, roll edge of ice cream in decoration in dish, gently pressing decoration into ice cream with your hand. If ice cream starts to melt too much, freeze sandwiches for a few minutes before decorating.

use your favorite flavor for filling!

COCONUT–PINEAPPLE PALETAS

Makes 6 paletas | Total Time: 15 minutes, plus 8 hours freezing time

PREPARE INGREDIENTS

1 (14-ounce) can coconut milk

1 cup (7 ounces) frozen pineapple chunks, thawed

3 tablespoons honey

1 teaspoon grated lime zest plus 1 tablespoon juice (zested and squeezed from ½ lime) (see page 16)

¼ teaspoon salt

GATHER COOKING EQUIPMENT

Blender

Dish towel

Rubber spatula

Fine-mesh strainer

Large bowl

4-cup liquid measuring cup

6 ice pop molds, about 3 ounces each

6 ice pop sticks

"IT WAS SO COCONUTTY!!"
-AMALIA AND AUDREY, 11 AND 12

130

START COOKING!

1 Place all ingredients in blender jar. Place lid on top of blender and hold lid firmly in place with folded dish towel (see page 38). Turn on blender and process until well combined, about 30 seconds.

2 Stop blender and scrape down sides of blender jar with rubber spatula. Replace lid and continue to process until smooth, about 30 seconds.

3 Place fine-mesh strainer over large bowl. Pour coconut-pineapple mixture through strainer into bowl. Use rubber spatula to stir and press mixture to push liquid through strainer into bowl. Discard solids in strainer.

4 Transfer coconut-pineapple mixture to 4-cup liquid measuring cup. Fill ice pop molds following photos, right. Place in freezer and freeze until firm, at least 8 hours or up to 5 days.

5 When ready to serve, hold each mold under warm running water for 30 seconds to thaw slightly. Slide paleta out of mold and serve.

EASY ICE POPS

The word paleta means "little stick" in Spanish, referring to the handle that runs through the center of this icy treat. But unlike American ice pops, which are mostly sugar, water, and food coloring, Mexican-style paletas contain any combination of fresh pureed fruits, nuts, herbs, and spices. Just blend, strain, and freeze—and you're ready to enjoy!

HOW TO ICE POP

1. Divide mixture evenly among six 3-ounce ice pop molds.

2. Insert 1 stick into center of each mold. Cover molds and freeze until firm, at least 6 hours.

131

HOT FUDGE SAUCE

Makes 2 cups | Total Time: 25 minutes

You can substitute 2 percent low-fat milk for the whole milk if you want.

PREPARE INGREDIENTS

- 1 cup sugar
- ⅔ cup whole milk
- ¼ teaspoon salt
- ⅓ cup unsweetened cocoa powder
- ¾ cup semisweet chocolate chips
- 4 tablespoons unsalted butter, cut into 8 pieces and chilled
- 1 teaspoon vanilla extract

GATHER COOKING EQUIPMENT

Medium saucepan

Whisk

Fine-mesh strainer

"THIS WAS SO GOOD IT DIDN'T NEED ICE CREAM!"
-HILTON, 8

START COOKING!

1 In medium saucepan, combine sugar, milk, and salt. Heat over medium-low heat, whisking gently, until sugar has dissolved and liquid starts to bubble around edges of saucepan, 5 to 6 minutes.

2 Reduce heat to low. Hold fine-mesh strainer over saucepan. Pour cocoa into strainer and tap side of strainer to sift cocoa into saucepan (see photo, right).

3 Whisk mixture until smooth. Turn off heat.

4 Add chocolate chips to saucepan and let sit for 2 minutes. Whisk until sauce is smooth and chocolate is fully melted.

5 Add chilled butter and whisk until all butter is melted and sauce thickens slightly, about 1 minute.

6 Add vanilla and whisk until well combined. Serve warm. (Sauce can be refrigerated in airtight container for up to 1 month. Gently reheat sauce in microwave, stirring every 10 seconds, until just warmed and pourable. Make sure not to heat it for too long or your sauce could separate.)

HOW TO REMOVE CLUMPS

Sifting removes any clumps from the cocoa powder and makes sure your hot fudge sauce is smooth, silky, and lump-free.

Hold fine-mesh strainer over saucepan. Pour cocoa into strainer and tap side of strainer to sift cocoa into saucepan.

WHO INVENTED THE ICE CREAM SUNDAE?

Fact: Hot fudge sauce is a classic sundae topping. But who invented the most delicious of frozen desserts—the ice cream sundae—in the first place?

This is actually a subject of much debate. Residents of the tiny town of Two Rivers, Wisconsin, believe the sundae was invented in 1881 by the owner of a local soda fountain, when a customer asked for chocolate sauce on top of their ice cream. But folks in Ithaca, New York, claim the sundae was invented in their city in 1892, when a shop owner served vanilla ice cream topped with cherry syrup and—of course—a cherry on top. (Before they topped ice cream, the sauce and syrup were used to flavor drinks, such as sodas and egg creams.) We may never know for sure where the first sundae was made, but one thing is for certain: Whoever invented the sundae gave the ice cream world something to celebrate.

STRAWBERRY SAUCE

Makes 1 cup | Total Time: 25 minutes, plus cooling time

You can use thawed frozen strawberries instead of fresh strawberries if desired.

PREPARE INGREDIENTS

3¼ cups (1 pound) strawberries

3 tablespoons sugar

GATHER COOKING EQUIPMENT

Cutting board

Chef's knife

Medium saucepan

Potato masher

Rubber spatula

> **"THIS SAUCE GOES REALLY GOOD WITH VANILLA ICE CREAM. SO SWEET AND FRESH."** -MOLLY, 11

START COOKING!

1 Working with 1 strawberry at a time, place strawberries on their sides on cutting board and use knife to carefully cut off tops with leafy green parts (see photo, page 29). Discard strawberry tops.

2 Transfer hulled strawberries to medium saucepan. Use potato masher to mash until fruit is mostly broken down (see photo, right).

3 Add sugar and use rubber spatula to stir until combined.

4 Bring strawberry mixture to simmer over medium heat. Reduce heat to medium-low and cook, stirring occasionally, until sauce is slightly thickened, 10 to 12 minutes.

5 Turn off heat and slide saucepan to a cool burner. Let sauce cool completely, 20 to 30 minutes. Serve. (Strawberry sauce can be refrigerated in airtight container for up to 2 days.)

HOW TO MASH STRAWBERRIES

Use potato masher to mash until fruit is mostly broken down.

A BERRY NICE TOPPING

How do two ingredients, cooked for just 10 minutes, transform from whole strawberries and grainy sugar into a thick, sweet, glossy ice cream topping? Mashing the strawberries with a potato masher is the first key—it releases the strawberry juices into the saucepan. Those juices contain a lot of water. As you cook the strawberry-sugar mixture, the sugar dissolves into the water in the strawberry juice, creating a sweet, strawberry-flavored syrup. Cooking also causes some of the water in the strawberries to evaporate. That helps make the strawberry sauce thick and pourable. And don't forget about those mashed whole strawberries! As they cook, the heat breaks down the cells in the strawberries, which makes them softer, but since they're cooked for only 10 minutes, they keep their chunky shape. We think you'll be berry pleased with the end result: a sweet sauce, studded with chunks of fresh strawberries, ready to pour over ice cream, waffles, pancakes, and more!

CHOCOLATE SANDWICH COOKIES

Makes 20 to 36 sandwich cookies | Total Time: 2½ hours

For an extra-chocolaty, extra-dark, extra-snappy cookie, we used a combination of black cocoa powder and Dutch-processed cocoa powder. If you can't find black cocoa powder, you can use ½ cup (1½ ounces) total Dutch-processed cocoa instead.

PREPARE INGREDIENTS

Cookies

- 1½ cups (7½ ounces) all-purpose flour
- ¼ cup (¾ ounce) black cocoa powder
- ¼ cup (¾ ounce) Dutch-processed cocoa powder
- ¼ teaspoon baking powder
- ¼ teaspoon baking soda
- ½ teaspoon salt
- ¾ cup (5¼ ounces) sugar
- ½ cup refined coconut oil, room temperature
- 2 tablespoons milk
- 1 large egg
- 1 teaspoon vanilla extract

Filling

- 4 tablespoons unsalted butter, cut into 4 pieces and softened (see page 14)
- 1 cup (4 ounces) confectioners' (powdered) sugar
- ½ teaspoon vanilla extract
- ⅛ teaspoon salt

> **" I LIKE THE CRUNCH OF THE COOKIE AND THE FLUFFINESS OF THE FILLING." -CALVIN, 13**

GATHER COOKING EQUIPMENT

Medium bowl

Whisk

Electric mixer (Stand mixer with paddle attachment or handheld mixer and large bowl)

Rubber spatula

Parchment paper

Ruler

Rolling pin

2 rimmed baking sheets

2-inch round cutter

Oven mitts

2 cooling racks

Quart-size zipper-lock bag

Scissors

START COOKING!

1 For the cookies: In medium bowl, whisk together flour, black cocoa, Dutch-processed cocoa, baking powder, baking soda, and ½ teaspoon salt. Set aside.

2 In bowl of stand mixer (or large bowl if using handheld mixer), combine sugar and oil. If using stand mixer, lock bowl into place and attach paddle to stand mixer. Start mixer and beat on medium-high speed until mixture is combined and fluffy, about 2 minutes. Stop mixer.

3 Use rubber spatula to scrape down bowl. Add milk, egg, and 1 teaspoon vanilla. Start mixer and beat on low speed until combined, about 30 seconds. Stop mixer.

4 Add flour mixture. Start mixer and beat on low speed until just combined, about 1 minute. Stop mixer. Use rubber spatula to scrape down bowl. Start mixer and beat on low speed until no dry flour is visible, 30 to 60 seconds. Stop mixer. Remove bowl from stand mixer, if using.

5 Use rubber spatula to transfer half of dough to center of large sheet of parchment paper on counter. Use your hands to pat dough into 5-inch circle.

6 Place second large sheet of parchment on top of dough. Use rolling pin to roll dough into 11-inch circle (about ⅛-inch thick), rolling dough between parchment.

KEEP GOING →

REFINED VS. UNREFINED COCONUT OIL

The popular chocolate sandwich cookies you'll find at the supermarket (hint: Their name rhymes with Floorio) are crispy and snappy all at once. To get that texture at home, we use coconut oil. There are two varieties of coconut oil available in most grocery stores: refined and unrefined. Refined coconut oil is made from dried coconuts and doesn't have a superstrong flavor or smell. Unrefined coconut oil, however, is made from fresh coconuts, so it tastes and smells like . . . coconuts! We love coconuts, but we don't want coconut-flavored chocolate sandwich cookies, so make sure you use refined coconut oil in this recipe.

→ **7** Slide dough (still between parchment) onto 1 rimmed baking sheet. Place baking sheet in refrigerator and refrigerate until dough is firm, about 30 minutes.

8 Repeat steps 5 through 7 with second half of dough, 2 more sheets of parchment paper, and second rimmed baking sheet.

9 While dough chills, adjust oven rack to middle position and heat oven to 350 degrees.

10 When dough is ready, remove 1 baking sheet from refrigerator. Slide dough, still between parchment, off baking sheet and onto counter. Gently peel off top sheet of parchment from dough and place parchment on now-empty baking sheet. Use 2-inch round cutter to cut out 20 to 24 cookies and transfer to parchment-lined baking sheet.

11 Place baking sheet in oven. Bake until cookies are very firm, 13 to 15 minutes.

12 While first sheet of cookies bakes, repeat step 10 with remaining dough to cut out 20 to 24 more cookies and place on second baking sheet.

13 Use oven mitts to remove first baking sheet of cookies from oven and place on cooling rack. Place second baking sheet in oven and bake until cookies are very firm, 13 to 15 minutes. Use oven mitts to remove second sheet of cookies from oven and place on second cooling rack. Let cookies cool completely on baking sheets, about 30 minutes.

14 If desired, you can reroll scraps of dough to make 20 to 24 more cookies, repeating steps 5 through 11.

HOW TO FILL CHOCOLATE SANDWICH COOKIES

1. Squeeze bag of filling to pipe small dollop of filling (about the size of a quarter) in center of each upside-down cookie.

2. Place cookies from second baking sheet on top of filling, right side up, and squeeze gently until filling is evenly distributed and almost reaches edges of cookies.

15 **For the filling:** While cookies cool, in clean, dry bowl of stand mixer (or large bowl if using handheld mixer), combine softened butter, confectioners' sugar, ½ teaspoon vanilla, and ⅛ teaspoon salt. If using stand mixer, lock bowl into place and attach paddle to stand mixer. Start mixer and beat on low speed until mixture is just combined, about 1 minute. Stop mixer.

16 Use rubber spatula to scrape down bowl. Start mixer and beat on medium-high speed until filling is light and fluffy, about 1 minute. Stop mixer. Remove bowl from stand mixer, if using.

17 Flip cooled cookies over on 1 baking sheet. Transfer filling to quart-size zipper-lock bag. Push filling to one corner of bag and twist top. Use scissors to snip ½ inch off filled corner of bag. Assemble cookies following photos, above, to make 20 to 24 sandwich cookies (or more if you rerolled the scraps). Serve. (Sandwich cookies can be stored at room temperature in airtight container for up to 1 week.)

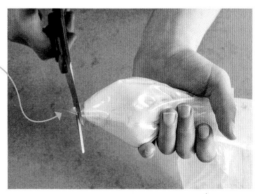

use a ruler to measure!

139

PEANUT BUTTER CUPS

Makes 24 mini cups | Total Time: 40 minutes, plus chilling time

You can substitute semisweet chocolate for the milk chocolate it you want. Make sure to use milk chocolate in bar form, not chocolate chips. If you do not have a mini-muffin tin, you can use a regular 12-cup muffin tin to make 12 larger peanut butter cups.

PREPARE INGREDIENTS

- 12 ounces milk chocolate
- ½ cup creamy peanut butter
- 3 tablespoons confectioners' (powdered) sugar
- 1 tablespoon unsalted butter, cut into 4 pieces and softened
- ⅛ teaspoon salt

GATHER COOKING EQUIPMENT

24-cup mini-muffin tin

24 mini paper cupcake liners (1 to 1¼ inches)

Large zipper-lock bag

Rolling pin

2 small microwave-safe bowls

Rubber spatula

Oven mitts

3 quart-size zipper-lock bags

Scissors

Ruler

" IT TOOK MY PEANUT BUTTER CUP EXPERIENCE TO A HIGHER LEVEL!"
-BEATRIX, 11

START COOKING!

1 Line 24-cup mini-muffin tin with 24 paper liners.

2 Place chocolate in large zipper-lock plastic bag and seal, removing as much air as possible from bag. Use rolling pin to gently pound chocolate into small pieces.

3 In small microwave-safe bowl, add half of pounded chocolate. Heat in microwave at 50 percent power for 1 minute. Use rubber spatula to stir chocolate. Return to microwave and heat at 50 percent power until melted, about 1 minute longer. Use oven mitts to remove bowl from microwave. Use rubber spatula to stir chocolate until completely melted and smooth.

4 Pour melted chocolate into one quart-size zipper-lock bag. Push chocolate to one corner of bag and twist top. Use scissors to snip ⅛ inch off corner of filled bag.

5 Pipe chocolate in spiral in each muffin-tin cup, working from outside in, to cover bottom of liner (see photo 1, page 143). Transfer muffin tin to freezer and freeze for 15 minutes.

6 Meanwhile, add peanut butter to second small microwave-safe bowl and heat in microwave until warm, about 1 minute. Use oven mitts to remove bowl from microwave.

7 Add confectioners' sugar, butter, and salt to warmed peanut butter and use clean rubber spatula to stir until well combined. Fill second quart-size zipper-lock bag with peanut butter mixture. Use scissors to snip ⅛ inch off corner of filled bag.

KEEP GOING →

HOLD ON TO THAT BAR!

Baking with milk chocolate chips is very convenient (no chopping or little bits of chocolate to clean up or, ahem, eat), but sometimes they won't act in the same way as a milk chocolate bar. Confusing, we know. Our favorite milk chocolate chips, while delicious, contain stabilizers. That means that when they melt, they turn gloppy and thick, rather than creamy and smooth. It's perfectly fine when you want the chips in your cookies or cakes to keep their shape, but for this recipe we turned to a milk chocolate bar for a smooth melted chocolate and great-looking peanut butter cups.

→ **8** Remove muffin tin from freezer. Pipe peanut butter mixture over chocolate layer in each muffin-tin cup in spiral to cover chocolate layer (see photo 2, right).

9 Add remaining pounded chocolate to bowl used to melt chocolate. Heat in microwave at 50 percent power for 1 minute. Use rubber spatula to stir chocolate. Return to microwave and heat at 50 percent power until melted, about 1 minute longer. Use oven mitts to remove bowl from microwave. Use rubber spatula to stir chocolate until completely melted and smooth.

10 Fill third quart-size zipper-lock bag with melted chocolate. Use scissors to snip ⅛ inch off corner of filled bag.

11 Pipe melted chocolate on top of peanut butter layer in each muffin-tin cup in spiral to cover peanut butter layer (see photo 3, right).

12 Transfer muffin tin back to freezer and chill for 30 minutes. Remove muffin tin from freezer and remove peanut butter cups from pan. Serve. (Peanut butter cups can be refrigerated in airtight storage container for up to 2 weeks).

HOW TO PIPE PEANUT BUTTER CUPS

1. Pipe chocolate in spiral in bottom of each muffin-tin cup, working from outside in, to cover bottom of liner. Take a break every six cups and gently tap pan on counter to even out layer of chocolate. Transfer muffin tin to freezer and freeze for 15 minutes.

2. Pipe peanut butter mixture over chilled chocolate layer in each muffin-tin cup in spiral to cover chocolate layer. Take a break every six cups and gently tap pan on counter to even out layer of peanut butter.

3. Pipe melted chocolate on top of peanut butter layer in each muffin-tin cup in spiral to cover peanut butter layer. Take a break every six cups and gently tap pan on counter to even out layer of chocolate.

CARAMEL APPLES

Makes 4 medium or 6 small caramel apples | Total Time: 40 minutes, plus chilling time

Freezing the caramels makes it easier to remove their wrappers. Tart apples such as Granny Smith are our favorites for this recipe, since they provide a nice contrast to the sweet caramel coating, but you can use your favorite apple instead.

PREPARE INGREDIENTS

1 (11-ounce) bag soft caramel candies (about 40 candies)

  Vegetable oil spray

4 medium or 6 small Granny Smith apples, stems removed

¼ cup heavy cream

½ teaspoon vanilla extract

¼ teaspoon salt

GATHER COOKING EQUIPMENT

Rimmed baking sheet

Parchment paper

4 to 6 popsicle sticks

Small saucepan

Rubber spatula

"IT WAS TASTY AND REALLY STICKY!"
-DAPHNE, 10

START COOKING!

1 Place caramels in freezer for 10 minutes. Meanwhile, line rimmed baking sheet with parchment paper. Spray lightly with vegetable oil spray. Set parchment-lined baking sheet next to stove.

2 While caramels freeze, insert 1 popsicle stick into stem end of each apple, pushing stick about 1 inch into apple.

3 Unwrap caramels and place in small saucepan. Add cream, vanilla, and salt.

4 Cook over medium-low heat until caramels begin to melt, about 5 minutes. Use rubber spatula to stir and scrape bottom of saucepan. Continue to cook, stirring often, until caramels are melted and mixture is completely smooth, 5 to 7 minutes. Turn off heat and slide saucepan to cool burner.

5 Working quickly, carefully dip apples to mostly cover with caramel, following photos, page 146. (If caramel becomes too thick to dip easily, reheat over medium-low heat, stirring often, until loosened, 2 to 3 minutes.)

6 Place baking sheet in refrigerator and chill until caramel is firm, about 30 minutes. Serve. (Caramel apples can be refrigerated in airtight storage container for up to 3 days.)

KEEP GOING →

A SHORTCUT TO SAFER CARAMEL

A true caramel is made by heating up sugar until it melts into a liquid and turns golden brown (a process called candying or caramelization). It's delicious, but also a little bit dangerous, as the sugar has to get **VERY** hot (over 350 degrees!), and it can burn you if it spills or bubbles out of the pot. This recipe uses soft caramel candies (which have already been caramelized for you) that you simply have to melt with a little bit of cream to turn into a safely dippable sauce.

try it this way
GO NUTS!

For extra crunch and flavor, you can add toppings to your caramel apple coating!

Place ½ cup finely chopped nuts (we especially like salted peanuts or pecans) or shredded coconut on plate and spread into even layer. Roll coated apple in topping before placing on parchment-lined baking sheet to set.

145

HOW TO DIP CARAMEL APPLES

1. Hold handle of saucepan and carefully tip to one side. Use other hand to hold popsicle stick and carefully dip apple into caramel, turning to coat most of the apple on all sides (ask an adult for help).

2. Lift apple out of caramel and gently shake to let extra sauce drip into pot, about 10 seconds.

3. Turn apple upright and gently twist back and forth to even out coating. Hold upright for 30 seconds to set coating.

4. Place apple, with stick pointing up, on greased parchment-lined baking sheet. Repeat dipping with remaining apples.

don't like granny smith apples?

use your favorite instead!

SPRINKLES

Makes about ⅔ cup sprinkles | Total Time: 1 hour, plus 8 hours drying time

Be sure to use gel food coloring—water-based food coloring will dilute the icing too much and your sprinkles won't hold their shape. The sprinkles come out best if you stick with only warm colors (such as red, yellow, and orange) OR only cool colors (such as blue, green, and purple). Mixing warm and cool colors results in a brown color. We used the Wilton No. 3 Round Decorating Tip to develop this recipe. Feel free to sub in another flavored extract for the vanilla. Peppermint, orange, lemon, root beer . . . anything goes!

PREPARE INGREDIENTS

1 cup confectioners' (powdered) sugar

¼ teaspoon vanilla extract

Pinch salt

4–6 teaspoons milk

Yellow gel food coloring

Pink (or red) gel food coloring (or your favorite colors—see note above)

" FUN! TASTED GOOD! A LITTLE MESSY."

-JOHN, 9

GATHER COOKING EQUIPMENT

4 rimmed or rimless
  baking sheets

4 pieces parchment paper

3 bowls (1 medium, 2 small)

Small rubber spatula

Pastry bag

Small round pastry tip
  (see note, page 148)

Scissors

Drinking glass

Bench scraper (or ruler)

Airtight storage container

START COOKING!

1 Line 4 baking sheets with parchment paper.

2 In medium bowl combine confectioners' sugar, vanilla extract, salt, and 4 teaspoons milk. Use rubber spatula to stir, scraping down bowl as needed, until smooth icing forms, 1 to 2 minutes (icing will be very thick). If icing is too thick to stir, add extra milk, ¼ teaspoon at a time, until icing becomes smooth.

3 Divide icing evenly among bowls, leaving one-third of icing in original bowl (you should have 3 bowls of icing). Use spatula to stir 2 to 4 drops yellow food coloring into 1 bowl of icing. Clean spatula before mixing next color. Stir 2 to 4 drops pink or red food coloring into second bowl of icing. Keep 1 bowl of icing white.

4 Prepare pastry bag with small round pastry tip, and fill pastry bag with white icing, following photos, page 19.

5 Pipe icing onto parchment-lined baking sheets following photos 1 through 4, pages 150-151, and re-filling pastry bag with yellow icing, and then pink or red icing.

6 Set baking sheets aside in cool, dry place. Let lines of icing dry at room temperature until they are fully hardened, at least 8 hours or overnight.

KEEP GOING →

A SPRINKLE BY ANY OTHER NAME . . .

Did you know that in England sprinkles are called "hundreds and thousands"? Maybe because they're so small, hundreds and thousands can fit into a container (or on your sundae)? And in Dutch, they are called hagelslag, which translates as "hailstorm," after their resemblance to the icy precipitation. What would you call these tiny, sweet, edible decorations if you could give them a new name?

→ **7** Once icing is fully dry, roll up parchment paper and gently break up icing lines into approximately ¼- to ½-inch sprinkles (see photos 5 and 6, right).

8 Turn parchment paper roll upright over airtight container, perpendicular to counter, and slide sprinkles into container. Serve. (Sprinkles can be stored at room temperature in airtight container for up to 1 month.)

HOW TO MAKE SPRINKLES

Don't worry if your lines aren't perfectly straight or if the line of icing breaks. As you use up the end of the white icing, the color will change at first to pale yellow and then, gradually, to bright yellow. This is called an ombré effect—the gradual blending of one color to another (you might have heard of it . . . in clothing, art, or even hair color!). The same will happen as you move from yellow to pink or red.

1. Hold pastry bag so it's standing straight up, perpendicular to baking sheet, with tip just above parchment paper. With 1 hand, squeeze pastry bag above twist to steadily push icing out of bag. At same time, move bag from one end of parchment paper to other end.

2. Continue piping lines of icing until you run out of white icing. You should pipe lines close together—just make sure they don't touch.

KEEP GOING →

3. Use bench scraper to push as much of white icing down toward tip as possible. Fill pastry bag with yellow icing.

4. Continue piping lines of icing across parchment, moving to second parchment-lined baking sheet when you run out of room on first sheet. Use all of yellow icing. Repeat filling bag and piping with pink icing. Let dry.

5. Once icing is fully dry, roll up parchment the long way (with icing lines facing inside). Use your hands to VERY gently squeeze parchment paper roll, breaking up icing lines into approximately ¼- to ½-inch sprinkles.

6. Turn parchment paper roll upright over airtight container, and slide sprinkles into container. Use bench scraper to scrape off any sprinkles stuck to parchment and scoop up any sprinkles that fell out and transfer them to container.

chapter 4

DRINKS

SIMPLE SYRUP

Makes 1 cup | Total Time: 10 minutes for plain simple syrup or 40 minutes for flavored syrups

Make sure to use a jar that has some extra room in it after adding the water and sugar— you need room for the liquid to move around as you shake the jar (otherwise the sugar won't dissolve). A pint- or quart-size jar works well.

PREPARE INGREDIENTS

- ⅔ cup sugar
- ⅔ cup water
- 1 flavored syrup ingredient (optional) (see Flavored Syrups, right)

GATHER COOKING EQUIPMENT

Jar with tight-fitting lid

Fine-mesh strainer
  (for Flavored Syrups)

Medium bowl
  (for Flavored Syrups)

" FUN AND EASY TO MAKE!"
— CALEB, 7

START COOKING!

1 In jar, combine sugar, water, and flavored syrup ingredient (if using). Cover jar with lid to seal. Shake jar vigorously until sugar dissolves, about 2 minutes.

2 Let jar sit on counter until syrup turns clear, about 5 minutes. If making a flavored syrup, let jar sit on counter for 30 minutes to infuse flavor, and continue on to step 3.

3 If making flavored syrup, place fine-mesh strainer over bowl. Remove jar lid and pour syrup mixture through strainer into bowl. Discard solids in strainer. Pour flavored syrup back into jar. (Simple syrup can be refrigerated in airtight container for up to 1 month.)

try it this way
FLAVORED SYRUPS

It's easy to flavor your simple syrup! Let herbs, spices, or fruits sit in the syrup to infuse it with flavor—just like when you steep a tea bag in water. Here are some fun options.

LEMON SYRUP	1 teaspoon grated lemon zest plus 1 tablespoon juice
LIME SYRUP	1 teaspoon grated lime zest plus 1 tablespoon juice
RASPBERRY SYRUP	1 cup raspberries (fresh or frozen and thawed)
STRAWBERRY SYRUP	1 cup quartered strawberries
PINEAPPLE SYRUP	½ cup pineapple chunks (fresh or frozen and thawed)
WATERMELON SYRUP	1 cup watermelon chunks
MINT SYRUP	1 cup mint leaves
GINGER SYRUP	½ cup chopped fresh ginger (no need to peel)

SO SIMPLE

To sweeten a cold drink, you could add a spoonful of sugar—but it won't dissolve all the way, leaving a grainy mess at the bottom of your glass. In simple syrup, sugar is already dissolved in some water, so it easily mixes into any drink. It's called simple because the formula is so easy to remember: equal parts water and sugar. You could boil water and sugar on the stovetop to make simple syrup, but our method is even simpler (and more fun): Just give it a good shake!

Vigorously shaking the sugar and water distributes the tiny particles of sugar in the water, which helps them dissolve. It also (slightly) increases the temperature of the mixture—the warmer the liquid, the more easily the sugar dissolves.

FLAVORED SELTZER

Serves 1 | Total Time: 45 minutes

If you're making flavored seltzers for friends and family, mix them one glass at a time. A big batch needs a lot more stirring, which means you'll lose those bubbles!

PREPARE INGREDIENTS

Ice

1 cup plain seltzer water

1 tablespoon Flavored Simple Syrup (see page 155)

GATHER COOKING EQUIPMENT

Glass

Spoon

" I LIKED IT EVEN BETTER THAN SODA AND MY MOM SAYS IT HAS LESS SUGAR." — JOSHUA, 9

START COOKING!

Place ice in tall glass. Pour seltzer water over ice. Add flavored syrup and stir gently to combine. Serve.

try it this way

There are SO MANY different flavors of seltzer you can make at home. Try making a few different syrup flavors (see page 155) and mixing and matching them! Here are some of our favorite combinations for flavored seltzers:

STRAWBERRY-MINT SELTZER

Use 2 teaspoons Mint Syrup (page 155) and 1 teaspoon Strawberry Syrup (page 155) per 1 cup of plain seltzer water.

RASPBERRY-GINGER SELTZER

Use 1½ teaspoons Raspberry Syrup (page 155) and 1½ teaspoons Ginger Syrup (page 155) per 1 cup of plain seltzer water.

PINEAPPLE-LIME SELTZER

Use 2 teaspoons Pineapple Syrup (page 155) and 1 teaspoon Lime Syrup (page 155) per 1 cup of plain seltzer water.

SELTZER, THEN SYRUP

When making your flavored seltzer, make sure to add the seltzer to the glass first, then the syrup. The syrup is denser and heavier than the soda, which means it will naturally flow to the bottom of the glass, which helps to gently mix your drink. If you made your drink the other way around (syrup, then seltzer), you'd have to stir more vigorously to mix them together, and you would wind up losing lots of your bubbles!

GRENADINE

Makes 1 cup | Total Time: 45 minutes

Allspice is a pea-size berry that grows on an evergreen tree in tropical climates. You can find dried allspice berries in the spice aisle of your grocery store. They have a warm spice flavor that tastes like cinnamon, nutmeg, and cloves.

PREPARE INGREDIENTS

8   allspice berries

¾   cup sugar

⅔   cup unsweetened 100 percent pomegranate juice

GATHER COOKING EQUIPMENT

Zipper-lock plastic bag

Small saucepan

Whisk

Fine-mesh strainer

Medium bowl

Jar with tight-fitting lid

" I LIKED MAKING THE SYRUP. I ALSO LIKED MAKING SHIRLEY TEMPLES FOR MY FAMILY."   - SOFIA, 7

START COOKING!

1 Place allspice berries in zipper-lock plastic bag. Seal bag, making sure to press out all air. Use small saucepan to lightly crush berries.

2 In small saucepan, combine sugar, pomegranate juice, and crushed allspice berries. Heat mixture over medium heat, whisking occasionally, until sugar has dissolved, about 5 minutes. Do not let it boil.

3 Turn off heat. Slide saucepan to cool burner. Let mixture cool completely, about 30 minutes.

4 Place fine-mesh strainer over medium bowl. Pour cooled mixture through strainer into bowl and discard allspice berries. Pour strained grenadine into jar with tight-fitting lid. (Grenadine can be refrigerated for up to 1 month.)

use it this way
SHIRLEY TEMPLE

Fill tall glass with ice. Pour 1 cup ginger ale over ice. Add 2 tablespoons Grenadine. Top with 1 maraschino cherry.

OMBRÉ COOLER

Fill tall glass with ice. Pour ⅓ cup orange juice, ⅓ cup pineapple juice, and 1 tablespoon lime juice over ice. Use spoon to stir together until well combined. Add 1 tablespoon Grenadine. Top with 1 fresh mint leaf.

ROY ROGERS

Fill tall glass with ice. Pour 1 cup cola over ice. Add 2 tablespoons Grenadine. Top with 1 maraschino cherry.

YUM... my favorite!

GRENADINE'S ORIGIN STORY

The word grenadine ("gren-ah-DEEN") comes from the French word for pomegranate, which is grenade (don't worry—these fruits are not explosive). Grenadine is traditionally made from sweet-tangy pomegranate juice, sugar, and sometimes flavorings such as allspice berries or rose water. However, when you see bottles of grenadine at the store, most of them don't contain any pomegranate at all! They're often made from a mixture of high-fructose corn syrup and natural and artificial colors and flavors—and they don't taste much like the real thing. Good thing it's easy to make this version (with real pomegranate juice) at home!

great drink to make with friends... it's so pretty!

WATERMELON AGUA FRESCA

Serves 4 to 6 (Makes about 6 cups) | Total Time: 20 minutes

PREPARE INGREDIENTS

- 8 cups (1-inch pieces) seedless watermelon (2½ pounds)
- 2 cups water
- ¼ cup lime juice, squeezed from 2 limes, plus lime wedges for serving
- 2 tablespoons honey
- ⅛ teaspoon salt
- Ice
- Fresh mint leaves (optional)

GATHER COOKING EQUIPMENT

Fine-mesh strainer

Pitcher

Blender

Dish towel

Rubber spatula

Glasses

> "IT WAS DELICIOUS! WE WOULD MAKE THIS AGAIN. MORE OF A SUMMER DRINK. BUT WE ENJOYED IT."
> — RONNIE, 13

START COOKING!

1 Place fine-mesh strainer over pitcher; set aside.

2 Add half of chopped watermelon and half of water to blender jar. Place lid on top of blender and hold firmly in place with folded dish towel (see page 38). Turn on blender and process until smooth, about 30 seconds.

3 Stop blender and remove lid. Pour mixture into fine-mesh strainer set over pitcher. Use rubber spatula to stir and press on watermelon bits to get out as much juice as possible. Discard solids in strainer.

4 Repeat blending and straining in steps 2 and 3 with second half of watermelon and water.

5 Add lime juice, honey, and salt to pitcher. Use rubber spatula to stir until well combined.

6 To serve, place ice in glasses and pour agua fresca over ice. Add lime wedge and mint (if using) to each glass. (Agua fresca can be refrigerated for up to 5 days; stir to recombine before serving.)

WHAT IS AGUA FRESCA?

Agua fresca means "fresh water." It is the name for a variety of drinks that are made by combining fruits, grains, seeds, or flowers with sugar and water. Some of the most common agua fresca varieties are horchata (made with rice and nuts) (see page 170), agua de Jamaica (made with hibiscus tea), and any variety of melon. We chose watermelon for our recipe and added lime juice, honey, and just a little salt to bring out the sweet and tart flavors. Serve it in a clear glass to show off that color!

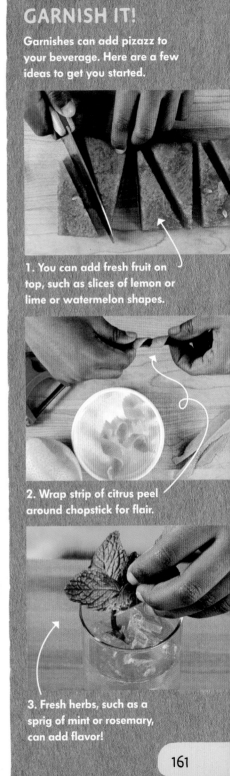

GARNISH IT!

Garnishes can add pizazz to your beverage. Here are a few ideas to get you started.

1. You can add fresh fruit on top, such as slices of lemon or lime or watermelon shapes.

2. Wrap strip of citrus peel around chopstick for flair.

3. Fresh herbs, such as a sprig of mint or rosemary, can add flavor!

161

FROZEN LIMEADE

Serves 4 to 6 (Makes about 6 cups)
Total Time: 25 minutes, plus 2 to 3 hours freezing time

PREPARE INGREDIENTS

7 limes
1 cup sugar
4½ cups cold water

GATHER COOKING EQUIPMENT

Cutting board

Chef's knife

Large bowl

Potato masher

Citrus juicer

Rubber spatula

Fine-mesh strainer

Large pitcher

2 ice cube trays

Blender

Dish towel

Glasses

"IT'S PERFECT FOR A HOT SUMMER DAY OUTSIDE."
– LILY, 11

162

START COOKING!

1 Cut 1 lime in half through both ends. Lay lime halves, flat side down, on cutting board, then cut each half crosswise into thin semicircles (see photo, right).

2 Add lime slices and sugar to large bowl. Use potato masher to mash sugar and lime slices together until sugar is completely wet, about 1 minute. Set aside.

3 Cut remaining 6 limes in half crosswise. Use citrus juicer to squeeze lime juice into bowl with sugar and lime slices.

4 Pour water into bowl and use rubber spatula to stir mixture until sugar is completely dissolved, about 1 minute.

5 Set fine-mesh strainer over large pitcher. Carefully pour mixture through strainer into bowl. Use rubber spatula to stir and press on limes to get out as much juice as possible. Discard lime slices in strainer.

6 Carefully pour half of lime mixture into 2 ice cube trays. Place trays in freezer and freeze until frozen solid, 2 to 3 hours. Place remaining lime juice mixture in refrigerator.

7 When limeade cubes are frozen, pop them out of ice cube trays and add to blender jar. Pour remaining lime juice mixture over top.

8 Place lid on top of blender and hold firmly in place with folded dish towel (see page 38). Turn on blender and process until smooth, 30 to 60 seconds. Stop blender. Pour into glasses and serve immediately.

try it this way
FROZEN RASPBERRY–LIME RICKEY

Add 6 tablespoons Raspberry Syrup (see page 155) to blender in step 7 along with lime juice mixture.

HOW TO SLICE LIMES

Cut lime in half lengthwise through both ends. Lay lime halves, flat side down, on cutting board. Then cut each half crosswise into thin semicircles. Discard ends.

MAKING A SLUSH

For this recipe we wanted a drinkable frozen treat like Del's Frozen Lemonade. We found that the best way to create a slushy frozen drink texture was to freeze half of our limeade mixture in ice cube trays and then blend it with the rest of the chilled liquid. Blending solid cubes with some liquid helps the cubes break down faster and create a slushy consistency. Another important factor in our slush-tastic drink? Sugar. The sugar in the limeade prevents it from freezing completely in the ice cube trays. And the slightly soft cubes are easier to blend into a slush!

BERRY-POMEGRANATE SMOOTHIES

Serves 2 (Makes about 3 cups) | Total Time: 10 minutes

PREPARE INGREDIENTS

- 1 ripe banana, peeled and broken into 4 pieces
- 1 tablespoon honey
- Pinch salt
- 2 cups frozen mixed berries
- 1 cup plain yogurt
- ½ cup pomegranate juice

GATHER COOKING EQUIPMENT

Blender

Dish towel

Rubber spatula

Glasses

"IT'S JUST THE RIGHT AMOUNT OF SWEETNESS AND IT TASTES REALLY GOOD!" – TRISTAN, 8

START COOKING!

1 Place banana, honey, and salt in blender jar. Place lid on top of blender and hold firmly in place with folded dish towel (see page 38). Turn on blender and process until smooth, about 30 seconds. Stop blender.

2 Remove lid. Add berries, yogurt, and pomegranate juice. Replace lid, turn on blender, and process for 30 seconds. Stop blender and scrape down sides of blender jar with rubber spatula. Replace lid, turn on blender, and continue to process until smooth, about 30 seconds longer. Pour into glasses and serve.

try it this way

Once you master the smoothie basics, the combinations are endless. Frozen fruit keeps things cold. If you have fresh fruit, place it in the freezer before you go to bed and wake up to frozen fruit!

GREEN MONSTER SMOOTHIES

Use 1 pitted avocado instead of banana. Use 1 cup frozen pineapple chunks and 1 cup chopped kale or baby spinach instead of mixed berries. Use ½ cup pineapple juice instead of pomegranate juice.

PEANUT BUTTER AND JELLY SMOOTHIES

Use 2 tablespoons strawberry jam instead of honey. Use 2 cups frozen strawberries instead of mixed berries. Use 1 cup milk instead of yogurt. Do not use pomegranate juice. Add 2 tablespoons peanut butter with other ingredients in step 2.

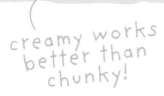

creamy works better than chunky!

You can blend up almost any fruit with some juice or yogurt and make a smoothie, but here are some tricks to making the best smoothies ever.

Make a creamy base.

Blending a banana or an avocado by itself first makes sure your smoothie is ultracreamy.

Bump up the flavor!

Adding honey and a pinch of salt brings out the natural sweetness in the fruit, making your smoothie extra tasty.

Use frozen fruit instead of ice cubes to keep your smoothie cold.

Ice will dilute your smoothie as it melts, but frozen fruit is full of flavor (and—bonus!—means there's no chopping or peeling to do).

Add yogurt, milk, or nut butter for extra staying power!

They have lots of protein that will keep you feeling full long after your last smoothie sip.

MANGO LASSI

Serves 4 to 6 (Makes about 5 cups) | Total Time: 20 minutes

We prefer this drink strained for a supersmooth finish, but the straining step is optional.

PREPARE INGREDIENTS

- 4 cups frozen mango chunks, thawed
- 2½ cups plain whole-milk yogurt
- 1 cup water
- 2 tablespoons honey
- 2 teaspoons lime juice, squeezed from 1 lime
- ⅛ teaspoon salt
- Ice

GATHER COOKING EQUIPMENT

Blender

Dish towel

Rubber spatula

Fine-mesh strainer

Large pitcher

Glasses

" I COULD REALLY TASTE THE MANGO."
- GAVIN, 9

START COOKING!

1 Add mango, yogurt, water, honey, lime juice, and salt to blender jar. Place lid on top of blender and hold firmly in place with folded dish towel (see page 38). Turn on blender and process for 30 seconds. Stop blender.

2 Remove lid and scrape down sides of blender jar with rubber spatula. Replace lid, turn on blender, and process until smooth, 30 to 60 seconds. Stop blender.

3 Set fine-mesh strainer over pitcher. Carefully pour half of mango mixture into strainer. Use rubber spatula to press and stir on mango bits to get out as much liquid as possible. Discard solids left in strainer. Repeat straining with remaining mango mixture.

4 To serve, place ice in glasses. Pour mango lassi over ice.

WHAT IS A LASSI?

Lassi is a traditional yogurt-based drink from India. Yogurt is blended with water, spices, and other ingredients. Lassis come in many varieties, with ingredients such as rosewater, coconut, papaya, cardamom, pineapple, and even salt. Mango-flavored lassis are popular all over the world!

try it this way
PINEAPPLE LASSI

Use 4 cups frozen pineapple chunks instead of mango chunks.

VANILLA MILKSHAKES

Serves 2 to 4 (Makes about 3 cups) | Total Time: 20 minutes

When making strawberry milkshakes, we like fresh strawberries, but you can substitute an equal amount of thawed frozen strawberries.

PREPARE INGREDIENTS

4 cups vanilla ice cream

½ cup milk

   Pinch salt

GATHER COOKING EQUIPMENT

2 to 4 glasses

Food processor

Rubber spatula

"THIS WAS LIKE DRINKING A CLOUD."

– ETHAN, 11

START COOKING!

1 Place glasses in freezer and chill until ready to serve. Remove ice cream from freezer and let sit at room temperature to soften, about 15 minutes.

2 Add softened ice cream, milk, and salt to food processor. Lock lid into place. Turn on processor and process for 30 seconds. Stop processor. Remove lid and use rubber spatula to scrape down sides of bowl.

3 Lock lid back into place. Turn on processor and process until smooth, about 30 seconds. Stop processor. Carefully remove processor blade (ask an adult for help).

4 Pour milkshakes into chilled glasses and serve immediately.

MAKING A GREAT SHAKE AT HOME

If you order a milkshake at a diner, it will probably be made with a special machine that makes milkshakes really light and frothy. The key to an awesome milkshake at home? A food processor! The bowl of the food processor is larger than the narrow jar of a blender. This means the ice cream mixture is exposed to more air, which helps keep the milkshake light. The food processor blade generates more heat than a blender, too, causing more of the tiny ice crystals in the ice cream to melt slightly, giving us a smooth milkshake!

try it this way

CHOCOLATE MALT MILKSHAKES

Add ¼ cup malted milk powder and 1 tablespoon unsweetened cocoa powder to food processor along with other ingredients in step 2.

STRAWBERRY MILKSHAKES

Use 2 cups ice cream instead of 4 cups and use ¼ cup milk instead of ½ cup. Hull 3½ cups (1 pound) fresh strawberries (see page 29). In step 2, add strawberries to food processor first. Process strawberries until smooth, about 1 minute. Then continue with step 2 as directed, adding remaining ingredients to processor.

SALTED CARAMEL MILKSHAKES

Increase salt to ¼ teaspoon. Add ¼ cup caramel sauce to food processor along with other ingredients in step 2.

COOKIES AND CREAM MILKSHAKES

In step 2, add 10 chocolate wafer cookies (broken into 1-inch pieces) to food processor first. Process until finely ground, 30 to 60 seconds. Then continue with step 2 as directed, adding remaining ingredients to processor.

HORCHATA

Serves 4 to 6 (Makes 5 cups)
Total Time: 25 minutes, plus 12 to 24 hours soaking time

Blanched whole almonds have had their skins removed. If you can't find them, substitute 1⅓ cups slivered almonds.

PREPARE INGREDIENTS

4½ cups water

1¼ cups whole blanched almonds

½ cup sugar

⅓ cup long-grain white rice

1½ teaspoons vanilla extract

1 teaspoon ground cinnamon

¼ teaspoon salt

1 cup evaporated milk

Ice

GATHER COOKING EQUIPMENT

2 large bowls

Plastic wrap

Fine-mesh strainer

Cheesecloth

Blender

Dish towel

Pitcher

Rubber spatula

Glasses

"MY BROTHER SAID IT TASTES JUST LIKE A SNICKERDOODLE!"
- REX, 12

START COOKING!

1 In large bowl, combine water, almonds, sugar, rice, vanilla, cinnamon, and salt. Cover with plastic wrap and let sit at room temperature for at least 12 hours or up to 24 hours.

2 When mixture is ready, set fine-mesh strainer over second large bowl. Line strainer with triple layer of cheesecloth that overhangs edges; set aside.

3 Carefully pour almond mixture into blender jar. Place lid on top of blender and hold firmly in place with folded dish towel (see page 38). Turn on blender and process until smooth, 30 to 60 seconds. Stop blender.

4 Carefully strain blended almond mixture through cheesecloth-lined strainer into large bowl, following photos, right.

5 Pour strained almond liquid into pitcher. Add evaporated milk to pitcher and use rubber spatula to stir until well combined.

7 To serve, place ice in glasses. Pour horchata over ice. (Horchata can be refrigerated for up to 3 days.)

HORCHATA HISTORY

Horchata's origin story begins more than 2,000 years ago, in ancient Rome, when people sipped on a drink made from a grain called barley. (The word horchata comes from the Latin word for barley, *hordeum*.) Over time, different cultures in Western Europe and North Africa adapted horchata recipes to use a variety of different grains and nuts, from almonds to sesame seeds to a vegetable called a *chufa*, or tiger nut. In the sixteenth century, horchata made its way to Mexico, where it became wildly popular. Today, the most popular recipe in Mexico for this cool and creamy drink is made from rice, sugar, and cinnamon.

HOW TO STRAIN HORCHATA

1. Carefully pour blended almond mixture into cheesecloth-lined fine-mesh strainer set over bowl. Let mixture drain completely, about 5 minutes.

2. Pull edges of cheesecloth together to form pouch, and twist top of cheesecloth to close tightly. Squeeze pouch over strainer to get out as much liquid as possible; discard solids and cheesecloth.

ALMOND MILK

Serves 4 (Makes about 4 cups) | Total Time: 20 minutes, plus 8 to 24 hours soaking time, plus 1 hour chilling time

Blanched whole almonds have had their skins removed. If you can't find blanched whole almonds, substitute 1⅓ cups slivered almonds.

PREPARE INGREDIENTS

1¼ cups whole blanched almonds

4 cups cold water, plus extra for soaking almonds

2 teaspoons sugar

½ teaspoon vanilla

⅛ teaspoon salt

GATHER COOKING EQUIPMENT

2 large bowls

Plastic wrap

Fine-mesh strainer

Blender

Dish towel

Cheesecloth

Pitcher

Rubber spatula

"IT SMELLED GOOD. IT WAS SMOOTH AT THE END."
— SELAH, 9

START COOKING!

1 Place almonds in large bowl and add enough cold water to cover by 1 inch. Cover bowl with plastic wrap. Let almonds soak at room temperature for at least 8 hours or up to 24 hours.

2 When almonds are ready, drain almonds in fine-mesh strainer over sink. Rinse almonds well.

3 Add almonds and 4 cups fresh water to blender jar. Place lid on top of blender and hold lid firmly in place with folded dish towel (see page 38). Turn on blender and process until almonds are finely ground, about 2 minutes. Stop blender.

4 Set now-empty fine-mesh strainer over second large bowl. Line strainer with triple layer of cheesecloth that overhangs edges.

5 Pour blended almond mixture into cheesecloth-lined fine-mesh strainer set over bowl (see photos, page 171). Let mixture drain completely, about 5 minutes.

6 Pull edges of cheesecloth together to form pouch, and twist top of cheesecloth to close tightly. Squeeze pouch over strainer to get out as much liquid as possible. Discard solids and cheesecloth.

7 Pour strained almond milk into pitcher. Add sugar, vanilla, and salt and stir with rubber spatula until sugar is dissolved. Place in refrigerator until cold, about 1 hour. (Almond milk can be refrigerated for up to 2 weeks; stir to recombine before serving, if needed.)

MILK FROM ... ALMONDS?

How do you . . . milk an almond? We know, it sounds weird. But almond milk—made from soaked, ground, and strained almonds—is a great nondairy alternative to cow's milk. Since many store varieties include thickeners, stabilizers, and gums, there's even more reason to make your own. It's important to soak the nuts for at least 8 hours so that your milk won't turn out grainy. Adding a tiny bit of salt and sugar rounds out the flavor!

chapter 5

DIY MIXES

This chapter is full of recipes for making big batches of dry mixes. You can store them in your kitchen, and make waffles or brownies or instant oatmeal whenever you like!

PANCAKE MIX

Makes 6 batches of pancakes (12 pancakes per batch)
Total Time: 10 minutes for pancake mix, 35 minutes for pancakes

PANCAKE MIX
PREPARE INGREDIENTS

10½ cups (52½ ounces)
       all-purpose flour

1⅓   cups (9⅓ ounces) sugar

5   teaspoons salt

6   tablespoons baking powder

1   tablespoon baking soda

GATHER COOKING EQUIPMENT

Extra-large bowl

Whisk

Fine-mesh strainer

Large airtight storage container

PANCAKES
PREPARE INGREDIENTS

1½   cups milk

2   large eggs

¼   cup vegetable oil

2   cups (10¾ ounces)
      Pancake Mix

     Vegetable oil spray

GATHER COOKING EQUIPMENT

Large bowl

Whisk

Rubber spatula

12-inch nonstick skillet

¼-cup dry measuring cup

Spatula

Serving plates or platter

START COOKING!

1 For the pancake mix: In extra-large bowl, combine flour, sugar, and salt. Whisk until well combined. Set fine-mesh strainer over bowl. Add baking powder and baking soda to fine-mesh strainer and tap side of strainer to sift mixture into bowl.

2 Whisk until very well combined, about 1 minute. Transfer pancake mix to large airtight storage container. (Pancake mix can be stored at room temperature for at least 2 months.)

TO MAKE ONE BATCH OF PANCAKES:

Before you start: Whisk the Pancake Mix inside the container to ensure that all the ingredients are evenly distributed (see "No Clumping," right).

1 In large bowl, whisk milk, eggs, and oil until combined.

2 Add 2 cups Pancake Mix and stir with rubber spatula until just combined (batter should look lumpy). Let batter sit for 10 minutes before cooking.

3 Spray 12-inch nonstick skillet with vegetable oil spray. Heat over medium heat until hot, about 1 minute.

4 Use ¼-cup dry measuring cup to scoop ¼ cup batter into skillet. Repeat 2 more times, leaving space between mounds of batter (you want 3 pancakes to cook up separate from one another).

5 Cook pancakes until bubbles on surface begin to pop, 2 to 3 minutes.

6 Use spatula to flip pancakes and cook until golden brown, 1 to 2 minutes. Transfer pancakes to serving plates or platter. Repeat with remaining batter in 3 more batches. Turn off heat. Serve.

PANCAKES FOR A CROWD

If you have an electric griddle, it's perfect for this recipe—just set the griddle to 350 degrees. You should be able to fit six pancakes in one batch. To keep batches of pancakes warm, set your oven to 200 degrees. As you finish a batch of pancakes, place them on a cooling rack set in a rimmed baking sheet and keep them in the oven while you make the rest of the pancakes.

NO CLUMPING

You will notice in these recipes for DIY mixes that we sift leaveners (baking powder and baking soda) and some powders (such as milk powder and buttermilk powder) before mixing everything together. These ingredients are very dry and powdery, so if there's any moisture, they can clump. This extra sifting step helps guarantee that there are no clumps and these key ingredients are evenly distributed throughout. If you notice any clumps once you've made your mix and you're ready to cook with it, measure out the mix you need for your batch and sift it one more time through a fine-mesh strainer before adding it to the bowl.

WAFFLE MIX

Makes 4 batches of waffles (four 7-inch round waffles or two 9-inch square waffles per batch)
Total Time: 10 minutes for waffle mix, 15 minutes for waffles

WAFFLE MIX
PREPARE INGREDIENTS

- 8 cups (40 ounces) all-purpose flour
- 1 cup (7 ounces) sugar
- ½ cup (2½ ounces) cornmeal
- 4 teaspoons salt
- ⅓ cup cream of tartar
- 2 tablespoons plus 2 teaspoons baking soda

GATHER COOKING EQUIPMENT

Extra-large bowl

Whisk

Fine-mesh strainer

Large airtight storage container

WAFFLES
PREPARE INGREDIENTS

- 1½ cups milk
- 2 large eggs
- 4 tablespoons unsalted butter, melted and cooled (see page 14)
- 2⅓ cups (13½ ounces) Waffle Mix

  Vegetable oil spray

GATHER COOKING EQUIPMENT

Waffle iron

Large bowl

Whisk

Rubber spatula

Dry measuring cups

Fork

Serving plates

START COOKING!

1 For the waffle mix: In extra-large bowl, combine flour, sugar, cornmeal, and salt. Whisk until well combined. Set fine-mesh strainer over bowl. Add cream of tartar and baking soda to fine-mesh strainer and tap side of strainer to sift mixture into bowl.

2 Whisk until very well combined, about 1 minute. Transfer waffle mix to large airtight storage container. (Waffle mix can be stored at room temperature for at least 2 months.)

TO MAKE ONE BATCH OF WAFFLES:

Before you start: Whisk the Waffle Mix inside the container to ensure that all the ingredients are evenly distributed (see "No Clumping," page 177).

1 Heat waffle iron. In large bowl, whisk milk, eggs, and melted butter until combined.

2 Add 2⅓ cups Waffle Mix and stir with rubber spatula until just combined and no dry mix is visible.

3 When waffle iron is hot, spray lightly with vegetable oil spray. Use dry measuring cups to pour batter into middle of waffle iron. (Use about ¾ cup batter for 7-inch round waffle iron or about 1½ cups batter for 9-inch square waffle iron.) Close waffle iron and cook until waffle is golden brown.

4 Use fork to remove waffle from waffle iron and transfer it to serving plate. Repeat with remaining batter. Serve.

WAFFLE IRON TIPS!

There are different sizes of waffle irons, so make sure that you know what size yours is before you start. When you pour the waffle batter onto the waffle iron, start in the middle and work your way out. You want to fill the waffle iron almost to the edges, but not all the way. If you overfill it, when you close the top of the waffle iron, the batter can overflow and spill over the sides!

CRISPY AND CREAMY

What makes a waffle different from a pancake? It's all about texture. Pancakes are generally soft and fluffy all the way through, but waffles should be crispy on the outside and creamy on the inside. To achieve that goal, this mix uses two unexpected ingredients: cream of tartar and cornmeal. Cream of tartar helps thicken the batter, which keeps the waffles custardy and soft inside, and a little bit of cornmeal adds crunch and crackle to the outside.

"I COULD FEEL MY STOMACH RUMBLING WITH HAPPINESS!"
~ DANIEL, 10

MUFFIN MIX

Makes 4 batches of muffins (12 muffins per batch)
Total Time: 10 minutes for muffin mix; 40 minutes for muffins, plus cooling time

You can use fresh or frozen blueberries or raspberries in this recipe; do not thaw if using frozen.

MUFFIN MIX
PREPARE INGREDIENTS

- 12 cups (60 ounces) all-purpose flour
- 4 cups (28 ounces) sugar
- 2 teaspoons salt
- ¼ cup baking powder
- 2 teaspoons baking soda

GATHER COOKING EQUIPMENT

Extra-large bowl

Whisk

Fine-mesh strainer

Large airtight storage container

MUFFINS
PREPARE INGREDIENTS

- Vegetable oil spray
- 1½ cups (12 ounces) milk
- 8 tablespoons unsalted butter, melted and cooled (see page 14)
- 2 large eggs
- 3¾ cups (22½ ounces) Muffin Mix
- 1½ cups blueberries, raspberries, chopped strawberries, or chopped bananas

GATHER COOKING EQUIPMENT

12-cup muffin tin	⅓-cup dry measuring cup
Large bowl	Toothpick
Whisk	Oven mitts
Rubber spatula	Cooling rack

START COOKING!

1 For the muffin mix: In extra-large bowl, combine flour, sugar, and salt. Whisk until well combined. Set fine-mesh strainer over bowl. Add baking powder and baking soda to fine-mesh strainer and tap side of strainer to sift mixture into bowl.

2 Whisk until very well combined, about 1 minute. Transfer muffin mix to large airtight storage container. (Muffin mix can be stored at room temperature for at least 2 months.)

TO MAKE ONE BATCH OF MUFFINS:

Before you start: Whisk the Muffin Mix inside the container to ensure that all the ingredients are evenly distributed (see "No Clumping," page 177).

1 Adjust oven rack to middle position and heat oven to 375 degrees. Spray 12-cup muffin tin with vegetable oil spray.

2 In large bowl, whisk milk, melted butter, and eggs until combined.

3 Add 3¾ cups Muffin Mix and stir with rubber spatula until just combined and no dry mix is visible. Gently stir blueberries into batter.

4 Spray inside ⅓-cup dry measuring cup with vegetable oil spray. Use greased measuring cup to divide batter evenly among muffin cups. (Muffin cups will be almost full.)

5 Place muffin tin in oven. Bake until muffins are golden brown and toothpick inserted in center of 1 muffin comes out clean (see photo, page 18), 20 to 24 minutes.

6 Use oven mitts to remove muffin tin from oven (ask an adult for help). Place muffin tin on cooling rack and let muffins cool in muffin tin for 15 minutes.

7 Using your fingertips, gently wiggle muffins to loosen from muffin tin and transfer directly to cooling rack. Let muffins cool for at least 10 minutes. Serve warm or at room temperature.

MAKE MUFFINS YOUR WAY!

This muffin mix makes a plain, lightly sweet batter that can work with lots of different flavors. The muffins bake up tender but sturdy, so they can handle having lots of berries or chopped fruit mixed in. To add a little extra flair to your muffins, try adding a pinch of warm spice (such as ground cinnamon, nutmeg, or ginger) to the batter when you add the fruit, swapping some of the fruit for chopped nuts or chocolate chips, or using a combination of fruits. Whatever you pick, just make sure to keep the total amount of mix-ins to 1½ cups or less. With this muffin mix ready to go in the pantry, you can make your muffins your way whenever inspiration strikes!

BUTTERMILK BISCUIT MIX

Makes 3 batches of biscuits (10 to 12 biscuits per batch)
Total Time: 10 minutes for biscuit mix; 35 minutes for biscuits, plus cooling time

You can find buttermilk powder in the baking aisle at most grocery stores, or you can order it online.

BISCUIT MIX
PREPARE INGREDIENTS

- 8 cups (40 ounces) all-purpose flour
- 4 teaspoons sugar
- 1 tablespoon salt
- 1 cup buttermilk powder
- 3 tablespoons plus 2 teaspoons baking powder
- 2 teaspoons baking soda

GATHER COOKING EQUIPMENT

Large bowl

Whisk

Fine-mesh strainer

Large airtight storage container

BISCUITS
PREPARE INGREDIENTS

- 1 cup (8 ounces) water
- 8 tablespoons unsalted butter, melted (see page 14)
- 2⅓ cups (12 ounces) Buttermilk Biscuit Mix
  - Vegetable oil spray

GATHER COOKING EQUIPMENT

Rimmed baking sheet

Parchment paper

Medium bowl

Whisk

Rubber spatula

¼-cup dry measuring cup

Oven mitts

Cooling rack

START COOKING!

1 **For the biscuit mix:** In large bowl, combine flour, sugar, and salt. Whisk until well combined. Set fine-mesh strainer over bowl. Add buttermilk powder, baking powder, and baking soda to fine-mesh strainer and tap side of strainer to sift mixture into bowl.

2 Whisk until very well combined, about 1 minute. Transfer biscuit mix to large airtight storage container. (Biscuit mix can be stored at room temperature for at least 2 months.)

TO MAKE ONE BATCH OF BISCUITS:

Before you start: Whisk the Buttermilk Biscuit Mix inside the container to ensure that all the ingredients are evenly distributed (see "No Clumping," page 177).

1 Adjust oven rack to middle position and heat oven to 450 degrees. Line rimmed baking sheet with parchment paper.

2 In medium bowl, whisk water and melted butter until combined.

3 Add 2⅓ cups Buttermilk Biscuit Mix and use rubber spatula to stir until just combined and no dry mix is visible.

4 Spray inside of ¼-cup dry measuring cup with vegetable oil spray. Use greased measuring cup to portion batter, following photo, right.

5 Place baking sheet in oven and bake biscuits until tops are golden brown, 12 to 14 minutes.

6 Use oven mitts to remove baking sheet from oven (ask an adult for help). Place baking sheet on cooling rack. Let biscuits cool on baking sheet for 10 minutes. Serve warm.

WHAT IS BUTTERMILK POWDER?

Buttermilk is the tangy liquid left behind when cream is churned into butter. Powdered buttermilk is made from that same leftover liquid—it's just dehydrated and turned into a powder. We use buttermilk powder here because it can be added to the mix as a dry ingredient. This way you can still make biscuits even if you don't have any liquid buttermilk in the refrigerator!

HOW TO PORTION

Spray inside of ¼-cup dry measuring cup with vegetable oil spray. Use greased measuring cup to scoop batter and use rubber spatula to scrape off extra batter. Drop scoops onto baking sheet to make 10 to 12 biscuits (leave space between biscuits and respray measuring cup as needed).

CORNBREAD MIX

Makes 4 batches of cornbread (each batch serves 12)
Total Time: 10 minutes for cornbread mix; 45 minutes for cornbread, plus cooling time

CORNBREAD MIX
PREPARE INGREDIENTS

- 6 cups (30 ounces) all-purpose flour
- 4 cups (20 ounces) cornmeal
- 2⅔ cups (18⅔ ounces) sugar
- 1 tablespoon salt
- 2 tablespoons plus 2 teaspoons baking powder

GATHER COOKING EQUIPMENT

Extra-large bowl

Whisk

Fine-mesh strainer

Large airtight storage container

CORNBREAD
PREPARE INGREDIENTS

- Vegetable oil spray
- 1 cup (8 ounces) whole milk
- 8 tablespoons unsalted butter, melted and cooled (see page 14)
- 2 large eggs
- 2¾ cups (17¼ ounces) Cornbread Mix

GATHER COOKING EQUIPMENT

8-inch square metal baking pan	Oven mitts
Large bowl	Cooling rack
Whisk	Butter knife
Rubber spatula	Cutting board
Toothpick	Chef's knife

START COOKING!

1 For the cornbread mix: In extra-large bowl, combine flour, cornmeal, sugar, and salt. Whisk until well combined. Set fine-mesh strainer over bowl. Add baking powder to fine-mesh strainer and tap side of strainer to sift baking powder into bowl.

2 Whisk until very well combined, about 1 minute. Transfer cornbread mix to large airtight storage container. (Cornbread mix can be stored at room temperature for at least 2 months.)

TO MAKE ONE BATCH OF CORNBREAD:

Before you start: Whisk the Cornbread Mix inside the container to ensure that all the ingredients are evenly distributed (see "No Clumping," page 177).

1 Adjust oven rack to middle position and heat oven to 375 degrees. Spray inside bottom and sides of 8-inch square metal baking pan with vegetable oil spray.

2 In large bowl, whisk milk, melted butter, and eggs until combined.

3 Add 2¾ cups Cornbread Mix and stir with rubber spatula until just combined and no dry mix is visible. Use rubber spatula to scrape batter into greased baking pan and spread into even layer.

4 Place baking pan in oven and bake until golden brown and toothpick inserted in center comes out clean (see photo, page 18), 25 to 30 minutes.

5 Use oven mitts to remove baking pan from oven (ask an adult for help). Place baking pan on cooling rack and let cornbread cool in pan for 20 minutes.

6 Run butter knife around edge of cake to release cake from pan. Use oven mitts to flip baking pan onto cooling rack to remove cornbread. Carefully turn cornbread right side up and let cool on rack for 10 minutes. Transfer cornbread to cutting board and cut into squares. Serve.

A TALE OF TWO CORNBREADS

Cornbread has been on the dinner tables of American families for a very long time. But there isn't just one type of cornbread. Over the course of American history, cooks developed two very different styles: Northern cornbread and Southern cornbread. Northern cornbread, which became popular in the states in and near New England, uses a combination of wheat flour and cornmeal and is sweetened with sugar (like this mix). It bakes up fluffy and a little bit cakey and is usually baked in a square or rectangular baking pan. Southern cornbread, which (no surprise!) became popular in the South, uses only cornmeal and usually has no sugar (or only a little bit). It bakes up a little denser, tastes more savory, and is usually baked in a round cast-iron skillet. There's a long-standing rivalry between these two styles of cornbread, but both are a delicious part of American history.

BROWNIE MIX

Makes 4 batches of brownies (16 brownies per batch)
Total Time: 10 minutes for brownie mix; 50 minutes for brownies, plus 1½ hours cooling time

We strongly recommend using Dutch-processed cocoa powder here. If you use natural cocoa powder, your brownies will be dense.

BROWNIE MIX
PREPARE INGREDIENTS

- 6 cups (42 ounces) sugar
- 1 cup (6 ounces) semisweet chocolate chips
- 4 cups (12 ounces) Dutch-processed cocoa powder
- 2 cups (10 ounces) all-purpose flour
- 1 teaspoon salt

GATHER COOKING EQUIPMENT

Food processor

Extra-large bowl

Whisk

Large airtight storage container

BROWNIES
PREPARE INGREDIENTS

- Vegetable oil spray
- 8 tablespoons unsalted butter, melted and cooled (see page 14)
- 3 large eggs
- 2½ cups (17½ ounces) Brownie Mix

GATHER COOKING EQUIPMENT

Aluminum foil

Ruler

8-inch square metal baking pan

Large bowl

Whisk

Rubber spatula

Toothpick

Oven mitts

Cooling rack

Cutting board

Chef's knife

186

START COOKING!

1 For the brownie mix: Add sugar and chocolate chips to food processor and lock lid into place. Turn on processor and process until mixture is combined and chocolate chips are coarsely ground, about 1 minute. Stop processor.

2 Remove lid and carefully remove processor blade (ask an adult for help). Transfer mixture to extra-large bowl. Add cocoa, flour, and salt to bowl.

3 Whisk until very well combined, about 1 minute. Transfer brownie mix to large airtight storage container. (Brownie mix can be stored at room temperature for at least 2 months.)

TO MAKE ONE BATCH OF BROWNIES:

Before you start: Whisk the Brownie Mix inside the container to ensure that all the ingredients are evenly distributed.

1 Adjust oven rack to middle position and heat oven to 325 degrees. Make aluminum foil sling for 8-inch square metal baking pan following photos, right. Spray foil with vegetable oil spray.

2 In large bowl, whisk melted butter and eggs until combined.

3 Add 2½ cups Brownie Mix to bowl. Use rubber spatula to stir until just combined and no dry mix is visible. Use rubber spatula to scrape batter into foil-lined baking pan and smooth top.

4 Place baking pan in oven. Bake until toothpick inserted in center comes out with few moist crumbs attached (see photo, page 18), 30 to 35 minutes.

5 Use oven mitts to remove baking pan from oven (ask an adult for help). Place baking pan on cooling rack and let brownies cool completely in pan, about 1½ hours.

6 Use foil sling to carefully lift brownies out of baking pan and place on cutting board. Cut into squares and serve.

HOW TO MAKE AN ALUMINUM FOIL SLING

Lining a baking pan with two pieces of aluminum foil makes it supereasy to get brownies and cakes out of the pan. For an 8-inch square pan, both sheets of foil should measure 8 inches wide and roughly 13 inches long.

1. Fold 2 long sheets of aluminum foil to match width of baking pan. Sheets should be same width for square pans.

2. Lay sheets of foil in pan so sheets are perpendicular to each other. Let extra foil hang over edges of pan. Push foil into corners and up sides of pan, smoothing foil so it rests against pan.

SUGAR COOKIE MIX

Makes 4 batches of cookies (12 cookies per batch)
Total Time: 10 minutes for cookie mix; 35 minutes for cookies, plus cooling time

You can find vanilla powder in the baking aisle at some grocery stores, or you can order it online.

COOKIE MIX
PREPARE INGREDIENTS

- 4 cups (20 ounces) all-purpose flour
- 3 cups (21 ounces) sugar
- 1 teaspoon salt
- 4 teaspoons vanilla powder
- 1 teaspoon baking soda

GATHER COOKING EQUIPMENT

Extra-large bowl

Whisk

Fine-mesh strainer

Large airtight storage container

COOKIES
PREPARE INGREDIENTS

- 4 tablespoons unsalted butter, melted and cooled (see page 14)
- 1 large egg
- 1½ cups (10 ounces) Sugar Cookie Mix

GATHER COOKING EQUIPMENT

Rimmed baking sheet

Parchment paper

Large bowl

Whisk

Rubber spatula

1-tablespoon measuring spoon

Ruler

Oven mitts

Cooling rack

START COOKING!

1 For the cookie mix: In extra-large bowl, combine flour, sugar, and salt. Whisk until well combined. Set fine-mesh strainer over bowl. Add vanilla powder and baking soda to fine-mesh strainer and tap side of strainer to sift mixture into bowl.

2 Whisk until very well combined, about 1 minute. Transfer cookie mix to large airtight storage container. (Cookie mix can be stored at room temperature for at least 2 months.)

TO MAKE ONE BATCH OF COOKIES:

Before you start: Whisk the Sugar Cookie Mix inside the container to ensure that all the ingredients are evenly distributed (see "No Clumping," page 177).

1 Adjust oven rack to middle position and heat oven to 325 degrees. Line rimmed baking sheet with parchment paper.

2 In large bowl, whisk melted butter and egg until combined.

3 Add 1½ cups Sugar Cookie Mix and use rubber spatula to stir and press mixture until soft dough forms and no dry mix is visible.

4 Use your hands to roll dough into 12 balls (about 1 heaping tablespoon each). Place dough balls on parchment-lined baking sheet, leaving space between them.

5 Use your fingers to gently press and flatten each dough ball into 2-inch-wide circle.

6 Place baking sheet in oven. Bake until edges of cookies are just beginning to brown and centers are still soft, 14 to 16 minutes.

7 Use oven mitts to remove baking sheet from oven (ask an adult for help). Place baking sheet on cooling rack and let cookies cool completely on baking sheet, about 30 minutes. Serve.

WHAT IS VANILLA POWDER?

With only a few simple ingredients, sugar cookies get a lot of their flavor from vanilla. In baking, we often use vanilla extract when we want vanilla flavor. Vanilla extract is usually made from vanilla beans, which come from special vanilla orchid flowers (it can also be made in a science lab!). To make vanilla extract, the vanilla beans are dried and then soaked in liquid. For our sugar cookie mix, we wanted vanilla flavor . . . without any additional wet ingredients! So we turned to vanilla powder. Vanilla powder is vanilla extract that has been dried out—a process that concentrates its flavor, making it especially vanilla-y. It's a great ingredient to use when vanilla flavor is the star—such as in yellow cake, vanilla pudding, or these cookies! If you can't find vanilla powder, you can add 1 teaspoon vanilla extract along with the melted butter and egg in step 2.

CHOCOLATE LAYER CAKE MIX

Makes 3 batches of layer cake (one 9-inch layer cake per batch)
Total Time: 10 minutes for cake mix; 1 hour for cake, plus 1 hour cooling time

CAKE MIX
PREPARE INGREDIENTS

4½ cups (22½ ounces) all-purpose flour

4½ cups (31½ ounces) sugar

3 cups (9 ounces Dutch-processed cocoa powder

1½ teaspoons salt

1 tablespoon baking powder

1½ teaspoons baking soda

GATHER COOKING EQUIPMENT

Extra-large bowl

Whisk

Fine-mesh strainer

Large airtight storage container

LAYER CAKE
PREPARE INGREDIENTS

Vegetable oil spray

1½ cups (12 ounces) milk

¾ cup vegetable oil

2 large eggs

3¼ cups (21 ounces) Chocolate Layer Cake Mix

Vanilla Frosting (see page 193) or your favorite store-bought frosting

GATHER COOKING EQUIPMENT

Two 9-inch round metal cake pans

Two 9-inch round pieces of parchment paper

Scissors

Large bowl

Whisk

Rubber spatula

Toothpick

Oven mitts

Cooling rack

Butter knife

Icing spatula

Serving platter or cake stand

Chef's knife

START COOKING!

1 **For the cake mix:** In extra-large bowl, combine flour, sugar, cocoa, and salt. Whisk until well combined. Set fine-mesh strainer over bowl. Add baking powder and baking soda to fine-mesh strainer and tap side of strainer to sift mixture into bowl.

2 Whisk until very well combined, about 1 minute. Transfer cake mix to large airtight storage container. (Cake mix can be stored at room temperature for at least 2 months.)

TO MAKE ONE 9-INCH LAYER CAKE:

Before you start: Whisk the Chocolate Layer Cake Mix inside the container to ensure that all the ingredients are evenly distributed (see "No Clumping," page 177).

1 Adjust oven rack to middle position and heat oven to 325 degrees. Spray inside bottom and sides of two 9-inch round metal cake pans with vegetable oil spray. Line each cake pan with 9-inch round piece of parchment paper.

2 In large bowl, whisk milk, oil, and eggs until combined.

3 Add 3¼ cups Chocolate Layer Cake Mix and use rubber spatula to stir until just combined and no dry mix is visible.

4 Use rubber spatula to divide batter evenly between parchment-lined cake pans and smooth tops. (Make sure to spread batter out to edges of each pan to create even layer.)

5 Place cake pans in oven. Bake until toothpick inserted in center of each cake comes out clean (see photo, page 18), 34 to 36 minutes.

KEEP GOING →

WHAT IS DUTCH-PROCESSED COCOA?

This recipe calls for something called Dutch-processed cocoa powder. What in the world?! And, is it different from regular unsweetened cocoa powder? Dutch-processed cocoa powder IS different than regular cocoa powder. It all comes down to how it's made. A process called Dutching, which was invented in the 19th century by a Dutch chemist and chocolatier named Coenraad van Houten, raises cocoa powder's pH level, which gives the cocoa a fuller flavor and deeper color. Dutch-processed cocoa (sometimes called alkalized or European-style cocoa) is the best choice for this recipe.

6 Use oven mitts to remove cake pans from oven (ask an adult for help). Place cake pans on cooling rack and let cakes cool completely in pans, about 1 hour. (This is a good time to make the frosting. See recipe, right.)

7 Run butter knife around edge of cakes to loosen them from pans. Remove cakes from pans and discard parchment. Assemble and frost cake following photos, right. Cut into wedges and serve.

HOW TO FROST LAYER CAKE

An icing (or offset) spatula, a large spatula with a bend in the blade, is best here, but a butter knife will also work.

1. Place 1 cake layer on serving platter or cake stand. Use icing spatula to spread 1 cup frosting over top of cake. Top with second cake layer and press down gently to set.

2. Use icing spatula to spread remaining 4 cups frosting over top and sides of cake. Use icing spatula to gently smooth out bumps around sides of cake and to tidy areas where frosting on top and sides merge. Then run spatula over top of cake again to smooth out any remaining bumps.

VANILLA FROSTING

Makes 5 cups (enough for 1 layer cake)
Total Time: 20 minutes

PREPARE INGREDIENTS

- 1 pound (4 sticks) unsalted butter, cut into 20 pieces and softened (see page 14)
- ¼ cup heavy cream
- 1 tablespoon vanilla extract
- ¼ teaspoon salt
- 4 cups confectioners' (powdered) sugar

GATHER COOKING EQUIPMENT

Electric mixer (stand mixer with paddle attachment or handheld mixer and large bowl)

Rubber spatula

START COOKING!

1 In bowl of stand mixer (or large bowl if using handheld mixer), combine softened butter, cream, vanilla, and salt. Lock bowl into place and attach paddle to stand mixer, if using.

2 Start mixer on medium speed and beat until smooth, about 1 minute. Stop mixer. Use rubber spatula to scrape down bowl.

3 Start mixer on low speed. Slowly add confectioners' sugar, a little bit at a time, and beat until smooth, about 4 minutes.

4 Increase speed to medium-high and beat until frosting is light and fluffy, about 5 minutes. Stop mixer. Remove bowl from stand mixer, if using.

INSTANT OATMEAL MIX

Makes 12 batches of oatmeal (1 cup per batch)
Total Time: 10 minutes for oatmeal mix, 5 minutes for oatmeal

INSTANT OATMEAL MIX
PREPARE INGREDIENTS

- 6 tablespoons sugar
- ¾ teaspoon salt
- ¾ teaspoon ground cinnamon
- 2¼ cups plus 2¼ cups old-fashioned rolled oats, measured separately

GATHER COOKING EQUIPMENT

Food processor

Large bowl

Rubber spatula

Airtight storage container

INSTANT OATMEAL
PREPARE INGREDIENTS

- ⅔ cup water
- ⅓ cup Instant Oatmeal Mix

GATHER COOKING EQUIPMENT

Microwave-safe serving bowl

Small microwave-safe plate

Spoon

Oven mitts

" I LIKED HOW THE OATMEAL HAD A CINNAMON TWIST TO IT."
- JAYDON, 12

START COOKING!

1 For the instant oatmeal mix: Add sugar, salt, cinnamon, and 2¼ cups oats to food processor and lock lid into place. Hold down pulse button for 1 second, then release. Repeat until oats are finely chopped and mostly broken down, about ten 1-second pulses.

2 Remove lid and carefully remove processor blade (ask an adult for help). Transfer mixture to large bowl.

3 Add remaining 2¼ cups oats to bowl. Use rubber spatula to stir until very well combined, about 1 minute. Transfer mixture to airtight storage container. (Instant oatmeal mix can be stored at room temperature for at least 2 months.)

TO MAKE ONE SERVING OF OATMEAL:

Before you start: Whisk the Instant Oatmeal Mix inside the container to ensure that all the ingredients are evenly distributed.

Combine water and ⅓ cup Instant Oatmeal Mix in microwave-safe serving bowl. Place small microwave-safe plate on top of bowl and heat in microwave for 1 minute. Use spoon to stir mixture. Continue to heat in microwave until mixture is thickened and liquid is mostly absorbed, 30 to 60 seconds. Use oven mitts to remove bowl from microwave. Serve. (Oatmeal will continue to thicken as it cools.)

BREAKFAST IN AN INSTANT

Instant oatmeal packets are a great quick breakfast. The key to the best instant oatmeal is the right texture. We used old-fashioned rolled oats—and left half of them whole and pulsed the other half in the food processor. The whole oats have nice chew, and the pulsed oats cook quickly in the microwave to add just the right amount of sticky-in-a-good-way texture. Bonus: Using the food processor makes it easy to add in dried fruit or nuts and easily chop them into small pieces for flavored oatmeal options. We use freeze-dried fruit in our variations because all its water has been removed, making it superflavorful. A scoop of this mix, a little bit of water, and 2 minutes in the microwave are all you need for a healthy start to the day!

try it this way

STRAWBERRIES AND CREAM INSTANT OATMEAL MIX

Increase sugar to ½ cup. In step 1 of Instant Oatmeal Mix, add 3 cups freeze-dried strawberries and 3 tablespoons nonfat dry milk powder to food processor along with sugar.

BLUEBERRY–ALMOND INSTANT OATMEAL MIX

Increase sugar to ½ cup. In step 1 of Instant Oatmeal Mix, add ¾ cup freeze-dried blueberries and ¾ cup slivered almonds to food processor along with sugar.

MACARONI AND CHEESE MIX

Makes 12 batches of macaroni (1 cup per batch)
Total Time: 10 minutes for macaroni and cheese mix, 25 minutes for macaroni and cheese

You can find cheddar cheese powder at some grocery stores, or you can order it online.

MACARONI AND CHEESE MIX

PREPARE INGREDIENTS

2½ cups cheddar cheese powder

½ cup nonfat dry milk powder

1 teaspoon dry mustard

GATHER COOKING EQUIPMENT

Large bowl

Whisk

Airtight storage container

MACARONI AND CHEESE

PREPARE INGREDIENTS

Water

½ cup elbow macaroni

1½ teaspoons salt

1 tablespoon unsalted butter

¼ cup Macaroni and Cheese Mix

GATHER COOKING EQUIPMENT

Medium saucepan

Liquid measuring cup

Rubber spatula

Colander

1-tablespoon measuring spoon

START COOKING!

1 For the macaroni and cheese mix: In large bowl, whisk cheddar cheese powder, milk powder, and dry mustard until very well combined, about 1 minute.

2 Transfer mixture to airtight storage container. (Macaroni and cheese mix can be stored at room temperature for at least 2 months.)

TO MAKE ONE SERVING OF MACARONI AND CHEESE:

Before you start: Whisk the Macaroni and Cheese Mix inside the container to ensure that all the ingredients are evenly distributed (see "No Clumping," page 177).

1 In medium saucepan, bring 2 quarts water to boil over high heat.

2 Carefully add macaroni and salt to saucepan. Cook, stirring occasionally with rubber spatula, until macaroni is al dente (tender but still a bit chewy), 8 to 10 minutes. Turn off heat.

3 Set colander in sink. Carefully drain macaroni in colander (ask an adult for help). Return drained macaroni to saucepan (be careful—saucepan will be hot).

4 Add butter, ¼ cup Macaroni and Cheese Mix, and 2 tablespoons water to saucepan. Use rubber spatula to stir until well combined and no dry mix remains. Serve warm.

MACARONI AND CHEESE FOR MORE!

We developed this recipe for Macaroni and Cheese to make a quick meal for one person. If you want to make it for a friend, sibling, or your whole family, this recipe can easily be doubled or quadrupled!

FOR TWO SERVINGS:

Keep the salt and the water amount to boil the macaroni the same.

Use 1 cup (4 ounces) elbow macaroni, ½ cup Macaroni and Cheese Mix, 2 tablespoons butter, and ¼ cup water.

FOR FOUR SERVINGS:

Keep the salt and the water amount to boil the macaroni the same.

Use 2 cups (8 ounces) elbow macaroni, 1 cup Macaroni and Cheese Mix, 4 tablespoons butter, and ½ cup water.

FRENCH ONION DIP MIX

Makes 5 batches of dip (1 cup per batch)
Total Time: 5 minutes for french onion dip mix, 20 minutes for dip

You can find beef bouillon powder in the spice or soup aisle at most grocery stores, or you can order it online.

FRENCH ONION DIP MIX
PREPARE INGREDIENTS

- ⅔ cup minced dried onion
- 5 teaspoons beef bouillon powder
- 1¼ teaspoons dried parsley
- ½ teaspoon garlic powder
- ½ teaspoon pepper

GATHER COOKING EQUIPMENT

Medium bowl

Whisk

Airtight storage container

DIP
PREPARE INGREDIENTS

- 1 cup sour cream
- 2 tablespoons French Onion Dip Mix

GATHER COOKING EQUIPMENT

Medium bowl

Rubber spatula

Plastic wrap

"IT WOULD TASTE GOOD WITH VEGETABLES. I TRIED IT ON A POTATO CHIP, TOO." – ELLA, 10

START COOKING!

1 For the French onion dip mix: In medium bowl, add minced dried onion, bouillon powder, dried parsley, garlic powder, and pepper. Whisk until well combined, about 1 minute.

2 Transfer mixture to airtight storage container. (Dip mix can be stored at room temperature for at least 2 months.)

TO MAKE ONE BATCH OF DIP:

Before you start: Whisk the French Onion Dip Mix inside the container to ensure that all the ingredients are evenly distributed.

1 In medium bowl, combine sour cream and 2 tablespoons French Onion Dip Mix. Use rubber spatula to stir until ingredients are well combined and no dry mix remains.

2 Cover dip with plastic wrap and place in refrigerator for 15 to 30 minutes before serving.

WHERE'S THE BEEF?!

In this recipe we use something called beef bouillon powder, which is basically a liquid beef stock that's dried out to make a superflavorful powder. It is typically mixed with water and used as a base for soups and sauces. Beef bouillon powder may seem like a weird thing to add to your French Onion Dip Mix, but there's a good reason for it! French Onion Dip is based on the flavors of French onion soup, which is made from onions and beef stock. Since we can't put liquid beef stock into our dip, we turned to beef bouillon powder. Bouillon is sometimes packaged in cubes, but we found cubes difficult to break up and add to our dip mix. Bouillon powder mixes easily with the other dried spices and incorporates evenly into sour cream to make our yummy dip!

HOT COCOA MIX

Serves 10 (Makes 3½ cups mix)
Total Time: 5 minutes for hot cocoa mix, 5 minutes for hot cocoa

HOT COCOA MIX
PREPARE INGREDIENTS

1½ cups nonfat dry milk powder

1 cup confectioners' (powdered) sugar

¾ cup Dutch-processed cocoa powder

¾ cup white chocolate chips

⅛ teaspoon salt

GATHER COOKING EQUIPMENT

Food processor

Rubber spatula

Airtight storage container

HOT COCOA
PREPARE INGREDIENTS

⅓ cup Hot Cocoa Mix

1 cup milk

Whipped cream (optional)

Mini marshmallows (optional)

GATHER COOKING EQUIPMENT

Large mug

Oven mitts

Spoon

"THE HOT CHOCOLATE MIXED AND MELTED BEAUTIFULLY!"
- TEGAN, 12

START COOKING!

1 For the hot cocoa mix: Add milk powder, confectioners' sugar, cocoa, chocolate chips, and salt to food processor. Lock lid into place. Hold down pulse button for 1 second, then release. Repeat until chocolate chips are finely ground, about ten 1-second pulses.

2 Remove lid and carefully remove processor blade (ask an adult for help). Use rubber spatula to transfer cocoa mix to airtight storage container. (Cocoa mix can be stored at room temperature for at least 2 months.)

TO MAKE ONE SERVING OF HOT COCOA:

Before you start: Whisk the Hot Cocoa Mix inside the container to ensure that all the ingredients are evenly distributed.

1 Add ⅓ cup Hot Cocoa Mix to large mug. Pour milk into mug over top of cocoa mix. Heat in microwave until hot, about 2 minutes. Use oven mitts to remove mug from microwave.

2 Stir with spoon until well combined. Top with whipped cream or mini marshmallows (if using).

TOP IT OFF!

There are SO many options for topping your hot cocoa. We suggest mini marshmallows and whipped cream, but don't stop there! You can also try sprinkles, grated chocolate curls (dark, milk, or white!), or even a candy cane stirrer.

HOW TO MAKE WHIPPED CREAM

For great whipped cream, heavy or whipping cream is a must. And make sure that the cream is cold. Use an electric mixer for the fastest results, although you can use a whisk and whip the cream by hand—just be prepared for a workout! If using a mixer, keep the beaters low in the bowl to minimize splatter. This recipe makes about 1 cup of whipped cream. (To make 2 cups, double all the ingredients.)

TO MAKE WHIPPED CREAM:

In large bowl, combine ½ cup cold heavy cream, 1½ teaspoons sugar, and ½ teaspoon vanilla extract. Start electric mixer and whip cream on medium-low speed for 1 minute. Increase speed to high and whip until cream is smooth and thick, about 1 minute. Stop mixer and lift beaters out of cream. If cream clings to beaters and makes soft peaks that stand up on their own, you're done. If not, keep beating for 30 seconds and check again. Be careful not to overwhip cream.

CONVERSIONS & EQUIVALENTS

The recipes in this book were developed using standard U.S. measures. The charts below offer equivalents for U.S. and metric measures. All conversions are approximate and have been rounded up or down to the nearest whole number.

VOLUME CONVERSIONS

U.S.	Metric
1 teaspoon	5 milliliters
2 teaspoons	10 milliliters
1 tablespoon	15 milliliters
2 tablespoons	30 milliliters
¼ cup	59 milliliters
⅓ cup	79 milliliters
½ cup	118 milliliters
¾ cup	177 milliliters
1 cup	237 milliliters
2 cups (1 pint)	473 milliliters
4 cups (1 quart)	0.946 liter
4 quarts (1 gallon)	3.8 liters

WEIGHT CONVERSIONS

Ounces	Grams
½	14
¾	21
1	28
2	57
3	85
4	113
5	142
6	170
8	227
10	283
12	340
16 (1 pound)	454

OVEN TEMPERATURES

Fahrenheit	Celsius	Gas Mark
225	105	¼
250	120	½
275	135	1
300	150	2
325	165	3
350	180	4
375	190	5
400	200	6
425	220	7
450	230	8
475	245	9

Converting temperatures from an instant-read thermometer

We include doneness temperatures in some recipes in this book. We recommend an instant-read thermometer for the job. To convert Fahrenheit degrees to Celsius:

Subtract 32 degrees from the Fahrenheit reading, then divide the result by 1.8.

Example
"Roast chicken until thighs register 175°F"

To Convert
175°F − 32 = 143°
143° ÷ 1.8 = 79.44°C, rounded down to 79°C

RECIPE STATS

Per Serving		Calories	Fat (g)	Saturated Fat (g)	Sodium (mg)	Carbohydrates (g)	Fiber (g)	Total Sugar (g)	Added Sugar (g)	Protein (g)
CHAPTER 1 - EVERYDAY STAPLES										
Peanut Butter	per 1 tablespoon	110	9	1.5	35	4	1	2	1	4
Chunky Peanut Butter	per 1 tablespoon	120	10	1.5	40	5	2	2	1	5
Chocolate Hazelnut Spread	per 1 tablespoon	90	7	0.5	10	7	1	5	5	2
Strawberry Refrigerator Jam	per 1 tablespoon	30	0	0	0	8	0	7	6	0
Blueberry Refrigerator Jam	per 1 tablespoon	35	0	0	0	8	0	8	6	0
Peach Refrigerator Jam	per 1 tablespoon	30	0	0	0	8	0	7	6	0
Raspberry-Chocolate Jam	per 1 tablespoon	40	0	0	0	10	1	9	8	0
Applesauce	per ½ cup	70	0	0	5	18	3	13	0	0
Ketchup	per 1 tablespoon	25	0	0	200	6	1	6	4	0
Barbecue Sauce	per 2 tablespoons	70	2	0	340	13	0	11	4	0
Hot Sauce	per 1 teaspoon	5	0	0	190	1	0	1	1	0
Sweet-and-Sour Sauce	per 1 tablespoon	60	0	0	45	14	0	13	0	0
Mayonnaise	per 1 tablespoon	130	14	2	80	0	0	0	0	0
Ranch Dressing	per 2 tablespoons	130	13	2	170	1	0	1	0	0
Balsamic Vinaigrette	per 1 tablespoon	110	11	1.5	100	2	0	2	0	0
Bread and Butter Pickle Chips	per ¼ cup	50	0	0	210	12	0	11	9	0
Pickled Red Onions	per 2 tablespoons	5	0	0	150	2	0	1	1	0
Basil Pesto	per 2 tablespoons	230	24	3.5	280	1	0	0	0	3
Fresh Tomato Salsa	per ¼ cup	10	0	0	160	3	1	2	0	1
Roasted Red Pepper Hummus	per ¼ cup	120	8	1	360	8	2	0	0	3
Lemony Herb Hummus	per ¼ cup	120	8	1	330	8	2	0	0	3
Butter	per 1 tablespoon	140	14	9	60	1	0	1	0	1
Ricotta Cheese	per 2 tablespoons	80	4	2.5	200	6	0	6	0	4
American Cheese	per 1 ounce	100	7	4.5	210	2	0	1	0	6
Everything Bagel Seasoning	per 1 teaspoon	10	1	0	140	1	0	0	0	0

Per Serving		Calories	Fat (g)	Saturated Fat (g)	Sodium (mg)	Carbohydrates (g)	Fiber (g)	Total Sugar (g)	Added Sugar (g)	Protein (g)
Pumpkin Spice Mix	per 1 teaspoon	10	0	0	0	2	0	2	2	0
Pumpkin Spice Butter	per ½ tablespoon	50	6	3.5	0	1	0	1	1	0
Pumpkin Spice Hot Apple Cider	per serving	130	0	0	10	31	1	26	2	0
Pumpkin Spice Cream Cheese	per 1 tablespoon	50	4.5	3	55	2	0	1	1	1

CHAPTER 2 - SNACKS

Per Serving		Calories	Fat (g)	Saturated Fat (g)	Sodium (mg)	Carbohydrates (g)	Fiber (g)	Total Sugar (g)	Added Sugar (g)	Protein (g)
Bagel Chips	per 5 chips	140	5	0.5	280	19	0	0	0	4
Garlic Bagel Chips	per 5 chips	140	5	0.5	280	19	0	0	0	4
Parmesan Bagel Chips	per 5 chips	180	8	2	450	19	0	0	0	8
Flavored Cream Cheese Dip	per 1 tablespoon	50	4.5	3	55	1	0	1	0	1
Pita Chips	per 5 chips	170	10	1.5	250	17	0	0	0	3
Buttermilk-Ranch Pita Chips	per 5 chips	170	10	1.5	430	19	0	0	0	3
Chili-Spiced Pita Chips	per 5 chips	170	10	1.5	280	17	0	0	0	3
Graham Crackers	per cracker	45	2	1	45	7	1	3	3	1
Cinnamon-Sugar Graham Crackers	per cracker	50	2	1	45	8	1	4	4	1
Cheddar Fish Crackers	per 15 crackers	110	8	5	105	6	0	0	0	3
Pizza Fish Crackers	per 15 crackers	110	8	5	110	6	0	0	0	3
Parmesan-Rosemary Fish Crackers	per 15 crackers	100	7	4.5	150	6	0	0	0	4
Seeded Crackers	per 5 crackers	160	9	5	340	17	1	2	2	3
Everything Crackers	per 5 crackers	150	8	5	430	17	2	2	2	3
Caramel Popcorn	per ½ cup	130	6	2.5	90	19	1	15	15	2
Nut and Seed Granola	per ½ cup	310	19	5	90	29	4	10	9	6
Nut-Free Granola	per ½ cup	300	18	5	90	30	5	10	9	7
Sweet and Salty Pepitas	per 2 tablespoons	100	8	1.5	140	3	1	1	1	5
Ginger-Soy Pepitas	per 2 tablespoons	100	8	1.5	75	2	1	1	1	5
Maple-Chili Pepitas	per 2 tablespoons	100	9	1.5	80	4	1	2	2	5
Cranberry-Almond Energy Bars	per bar	240	12	1	50	32	5	25	0	5
Strawberry Pop Tarts	per pop tart	390	19	12	300	49	0	20	2	5
Triple-Berry Fruit Leather	per strip	60	0	0	0	14	3	10	4	1
Strawberry Fruit Leather	per strip	50	0	0	0	13	2	10	4	0
Raspberry Fruit Leather	per strip	60	0	0	0	15	4	10	4	1

	Per Serving	Calories	Fat (g)	Saturated Fat (g)	Sodium (mg)	Carbohydrates (g)	Fiber (g)	Total Sugar (g)	Added Sugar (g)	Protein (g)
Chewy Lemonade Fruit Snacks	per 12 gummies	60	0	0	5	14	0	12	1	2
Parmesan Twists	per twist	90	7	3.5	150	8	0	0	0	3

CHAPTER 3 - SWEET TREATS

	Per Serving	Calories	Fat (g)	Saturated Fat (g)	Sodium (mg)	Carbohydrates (g)	Fiber (g)	Total Sugar (g)	Added Sugar (g)	Protein (g)
Vanilla No-Churn Ice Cream	per ½ cup	380	25	16	150	35	0	35	12	5
Mint Cookie No-Churn Ice Cream	per ½ cup	400	26	16	170	39	0	37	12	5
Milk Chocolate No-Churn Ice Cream	per ½ cup	490	32	20	160	47	1	45	22	7
Peanut Butter Cup No-Churn Ice Cream	per ½ cup	500	35	18	240	40	1	39	14	9
Strawberry Buttermilk No-Churn Ice Cream	per ½ cup	410	25	16	160	44	0	43	12	5
Raspberry Sorbet	per ½ cup	170	0	0	40	43	5	37	34	1
Blackberry Sorbet	per ½ cup	160	0	0	40	41	4	37	34	1
Ice Cream Sandwiches	per cookie sandwich	350	16	10	180	48	0	36	33	4
Coconut-Pineapple Paletas	per paleta	180	14	12	105	15	0	9	8	2
Hot Fudge Sauce	per 2 tablespoons	120	6	3.5	40	19	0	17	17	1
Strawberry Sauce	per 2 tablespoons	35	0	0	0	9	1	7	5	0
Chocolate Sandwich Cookies	per cookie	90	4.5	4	55	12	0	8	7	1
Peanut Butter Cups	per cup	120	8	3.5	45	10	0	9	1	2
Caramel Apples	per apple	260	6	2.5	170	50	4	40	20	3
Sprinkles	per 1 teaspoon	15	0	0	0	4	0	4	3	0

CHAPTER 4 - DRINKS

	Per Serving	Calories	Fat (g)	Saturated Fat (g)	Sodium (mg)	Carbohydrates (g)	Fiber (g)	Total Sugar (g)	Added Sugar (g)	Protein (g)
Simple Syrup	per 1 tablespoon	35	0	0	0	8	0	8	8	0
Flavored Syrups	per 1 tablespoon	35	0	0	0	8	0	8	8	0
Flavored Seltzer										
Strawberry-Mint Seltzer	per serving	35	0	0	50	8	0	8	8	0
Raspberry-Ginger Seltzer	per serving	35	0	0	50	8	0	8	8	0
Pineapple-Lime Seltzer	per serving	35	0	0	50	8	0	8	8	0
Grenadine	per 2 tablespoons	90	0	0	0	22	0	22	19	0
Shirley Temple	per serving	180	0	0	35	48	0	46	42	0
Ombré Cooler	per serving	130	0	0	0	32	0	26	9	1
Roy Rogers	per serving	200	0	0	10	51	0	49	19	0
Watermelon Agua Fresca	per serving	80	0	0	55	21	1	17	5	1

Per Serving		Calories	Fat (g)	Saturated Fat (g)	Sodium (mg)	Carbohydrates (g)	Fiber (g)	Total Sugar (g)	Added Sugar (g)	Protein (g)
Frozen Limeade	per serving	140	0	0	5	37	0	34	34	0
Frozen Raspberry-Lime Rickey	per serving	170	0	0	5	45	0	43	42	0
Berry-Pomegrante Smoothies	per serving	260	5	2.5	130	55	6	40	8	6
Green Monster Smoothies	per serving	350	19	4.5	140	44	8	23	8	8
Peanut Butter and Jelly Smoothies	per serving	330	12	4	200	50	6	34	0	8
Mango Lassi	per serving	160	3.5	2	95	30	2	27	5	4
Pineapple Lassi	per serving	140	3.5	2	95	25	2	21	5	4
Vanilla Milkshakes	per serving	290	16	10	120	33	0	29	22	6
Chocolate Malt Milkshakes	per serving	320	16	10	150	37	0	32	22	7
Strawberry Milkshakes	per serving	190	8	5	60	26	3	21	11	4
Salted Caramel Milkshakes	per serving	360	17	11	290	45	0	36	22	6
Cookies and Cream Milkshakes	per serving	360	18	10	210	44	0	35	22	7
Horchata	per serving	170	6	2	150	24	1	21	17	4
Almond Milk	per serving	60	5	0	80	4	1	3	2	2

CHAPTER 5 - DIY MIXES

		Calories	Fat (g)	Saturated Fat (g)	Sodium (mg)	Carbohydrates (g)	Fiber (g)	Total Sugar (g)	Added Sugar (g)	Protein (g)
Pancake Mix	per 2 pancakes	290	13	3	690	35	0	10	7	8
Waffle Mix	per waffle	460	16	9	820	64	0	17	13	12
Muffin Mix	per muffin	270	9	6	280	42	0	20	17	5
Buttermilk Biscuit Mix	per biscuit	170	8	5	410	21	0	2	0	4
Cornbread Mix	per serving	210	9	5	240	30	1	12	11	4
Brownie Mix	per brownie	180	8	5	50	25	0	20	20	3
Sugar Cookie Mix	per cookie	120	4	2.5	80	20	0	13	13	2
Chocolate Layer Cake Mix	per serving	460	29	14	160	48	0	40	39	3
Vanilla Frosting	per 2 tablespoons	130	9	6	15	12	0	12	12	0
Instant Oatmeal Mix	per serving	170	3	0.5	150	31	4	7	6	4
Strawberries and Cream Instant Oatmeal Mix	per serving	190	3	0.5	170	38	5	11	8	5
Blueberry-Almond Instant Oatmeal Mix	per serving	220	6	1	150	37	5	10	8	6
Macaroni and Cheese Mix	per serving	460	24	14	640	43	0	2	0	17
French Onion Dip Mix	per 2 tablespoons	50	4.5	2.5	115	2	0	1	0	1
Hot Cocoa Mix	per serving	290	10	6	390	39	0	36	12	14